MEMORIES

FROM A WAR

Volume I

A STOLEN YOUTH

ALOYSIUS PAPPERT

First Edition
2016

MEMORIES FROM A WAR
Volume I
"A Stolen Youth"
by Aloysius Pappert

Translated from the author's original French language manuscript by Wolfgang Mack. IP rights reserved.
English version edited by Francesca Mack
Cover design©and images by XTOF Designs
Back cover image by the author

Library of Congress Cataloging-in-Publication Data:
Library of Congress Control Number: 2016942751
ISBN-13: 978-1532861444
ISBN-10: 1532861443
BISAC:Biography and Autobiography/Personal Memoirs/ Religion

Published by WAMFAM Press
Seattle, Washington, USA
Printed in the USA

Also by the Author:
MEMORIES FROM AFTER THE WAR
Volume II
"The Blood of the Prisoners"

A Stolen Youth

Dedication

My memories of the war of 1939 to 1945 are dedicated to all my comrades in arms of all origins, nationalities or races, and regardless of the cause for which they fought. To all the young people of the world, that they never forget that freedom is the most precious thing of our life, and the love for country and our neighbors must always triumph over hateful propaganda.

Foreword

My long-time friend Aloysius Pappert writes movingly about his coming of age in Nazi Germany and his journey from boyhood through the inferno of World War II. Brought up in a tight-knit Catholic family he was imbued with the high moral values of his Church, never losing faith in God's guidance even in the most challenging times of utter disasters. That same set of values also gave him his keen sense of responsibility for his own irreproachable conduct in the depth of the war as a young Wehrmacht officer and in his never failing efforts to do everything possible for the safety and hopeful survival of the soldiers under his command.

Just like millions of young men all over the world he did not want to go to war, and like millions of men in other countries he had no choice in the matter. He just had to make the best of many bad situations. A Lieutenant at the young age of 20 his courage and his maturity were an inspiration to his soldiers to deal with the most horrific combat conditions where he had to witness more vicious fighting than anyone I know. All along he saw the demoralizing effects of the evil of the Nazi dictatorship whose cruelties had gripped his country and so much of the world and for which the Germans would eventually have to pay such a horrific price.

Aloysius' astounding talent for narrating his amazing experiences makes for fascinating reading. It is by far the best chronicle I know about a terrible period in recent history when much of the world was on fire, a time of ruthless fighting and the most horrendeous crimes committed in the name of the Nazi's godless ideology. Beyond that, however, his book is a timeless testimony to the power of the human spirit - and the strenght of his Faith.

VICE-ADMIRAL FREDERIC MAURICE, COMMANDER OF THE FRENCH NAVY IN THE PACIFIC (RET.)

A Stolen Youth

Young Aloysius Pappert at age 18,
drafted into the Wehrmacht
January 1943

Chapter 1

The National Work Service

Here I was, standing alone, a mere seventeen years old, for the first time so far away from my family. Here everything started for me, in front of the military barracks of Glauchau, 200 miles from home. In other times it would have been a call to military service. I might have been left with a light heart, with the idea of discovering a new life, making new friends. I was young and, of course, I knew that I still had a lot of growing up to do but I did not have the faintest ideas of all the ordeals that were waiting for me in the years ahead.

In March 1942, in a country at war for more than two years I was drafted into the 'RAD', the 'National Labor Service'. I was to spend six months doing hard physical labor in support of the war effort, one of the inventions of the Führer who, in so little time, had upset everything in Germany.

Since 1935, all young men of 18 and above were summoned to this service, really a paramilitary National Socialist meant to educate us youngsters on manual hard work of all kinds, roads, earthworks and structural work. Young girls were inducted into the 'BDM', the League of German Girls. In theory, they would train in paramedical work, but in practice many of them were to mate with young SS selected according to the criteria of the Nazi ideologues, and become future mothers to create a new race of people, a 'super race'. After their first delivery these women would stay another year to give birth to a second child. Once they had done that, these mothers would leave their offsprings in a Nazi education service.

Not all did, but I remember very well the day when the daughter of one of our neighbors had returned from her 'training' with two children, Helga and Helmut. As for the girls who had not been selected to become 'nurse' they were to toil six months at a farm with the usual dose of brainwashing in Nazi and anti-religious doctrine. The Nazi control over body and mind had become absolute, but what drove all this nonsense?

*

Who was this terrible leader who was in all our adult conversations? One day I was finally able to see his picture in a newspaper. Yikes! So that was Adolf Hitler? A kind of weakling, neither big nor strong, nor blond with blue eyes. He lived quietly in his lair in Berchtesgaden sporting his ridiculous Bavarian suit. Beside him my father looked like a Hercules with his six feet plus! For the boy that I was, there was something incomprehensible. "The devil does not need muscles" I had just said to my father. For him it was not a joke. I already knew his aversion to the "Führer".

In January 1933, all students received a small paper swastika flag. Our teachers had asked us to celebrate the new 'National Socialist' Germany with our parents the same evening. I returned like other children, waving the little flag, but my father took it from my hands and tore it to pieces. "You don't understand yet, but you will later" he explained to me.

From that day, Germany was about to change. The Nazi reign of terror against Catholics and all Christians put us in the regime's cross-hairs. My father was an outspoken critic of the new regime.

He made me promise never to speak to any one of our lives at home, not at school, to my friends, or to neighbors. Keep quiet. A lesson he would repeat over and over.

In April 1933 my father was arrested and taken to the Buchenwald concentration camp where he underwent two months of 'interrogation'. Thanks to the intervention of his friend, our school principal Willy Unverzagt, he was released, but now under constant surveillance, marked as an enemy of the regime. He was an influential member of the Catholic Center Party of Germany, on the board of the Raiffeisen Bank and on the municipal council. He was a prominent figure in the region. I knew he had not fought in the 1914 war because of a heart problem. In return for being exempt from military service he had to expand his saddlery and upholstery business to work exclusively for the military. Towards the end of the First World War, he employed over thirty people including French prisoners who were living in the shop annex. My mother cooked for all of them with the help of other women. Despite his loyalty to Emperor William II, my father had a hard time to accept that Germany had been drawn into that war by the Austro-Hungarian Empire for which he had no sympathy.

After his first arrest, professional ostracism followed. The Nazis had withdrawn his trade license because he refused to join the German Labor Front, the single national union which, of course, was entirely under the control of the Nazis. So he asked my brother Josef, ten years my senior, to put his name on our upholstery workshop. On paper, my father became the employee of his son at the time when Josef had just returned from his military service. He had participated in the German invasion into the demilitarized zone in the West, in violation of the Versailles Treaty. He told us how his company, stationed in Rastatt just across the bridge from Strasbourg, was ordered to back off if the French army responded as was feared, as they were much stronger militarily. The French army limited itself to observing the advancing Germans, and a few days later, even exchanging a few friendly words with them. The German army had been able to quietly take over its neighboring areas.

For my father, it was appalling. The coming to power of the Nazis had overwhelmed him. He had seen the Nazi ideas seeping in everywhere, even under our roof. One example was my brother, Josef, who was about twenty years old when one evening he had entered the house in the uniform of the SA, Hitler's private political army. Josef was then employed by the railways and Nazi propaganda was very active in the railways. He was seduced by a speech of the Fuhrer, and he had approached the first Nazis established in our region. Seeing him in this uniform, my father immediately asked him to change, but Josef had slammed the door and left. He had never acted like this. He returned two days later, in plain clothes.

My father was probably one of the first anti-Nazis to actually have read, very carefully, the Nazis's bible, 'Mein Kampf'. He had taken it very seriously unlike others who saw it as ravings of a fanatic.

There were several Jews among his suppliers. Early on, he showed them Hitler's book, saying: "Look, it's in black and white: Jews, Christians, gypsies and all the 'sub humans' will be wiped off the face of the earth." Sometimes his words had been heeded and as a result some of his Jewish friends had sold their business and left Germany in time.

There was Mr. Hirsch from Kassel, a Jewish wholesale supplier of leather in all its forms. He had served in the Great War attaining the rank of colonel. His heroic conduct earned him the highest honor of the German army: the Grand Cross of Merit. I remember him well, his bursts of laughter and always some candy emerging from his pocket for my sister and me. This man was unable to imagine for a moment that Hitler ever would harm a German like himself, his 'brother-in-arms'. He did not hesitate to take part in a parade before the Führer in Berlin with other officers and generals of the former German army. He told my father before Kristallnacht he had been warned of the imminence of the attack on his business and that the S.A. would come to invade his factory. To greet them he donned his uniform of colonel with its decoration. Firmly camped outside his factory he confronted the SA, pointing his pistol in the air and shouting: "You gangs of thugs, lazy bums, leave here immediately and never come back, or I will ask my army friend, Adolf Hitler, to stop you!" Nothing further had happened.

I eagerly listened to the discussions of the grown-ups, especially my father and his friend, the school principal, who had been forced like all civil servants to join the Nazi party just to keep his job. Thanks to him my father had an ally in place: Willy Unverzagt, who never identified with the Nazis. My father made him subscribe to the "Stürmer", the most virulent and most anti-Semitic newspapers, just for showing an interest in the intentions of the regime. My father never uttered the name of Hitler. He did not call him anything but "that Austrian corporal". The "Austrian corporal" wanted war and he would not have any one stop him.

*

It was on September 1, 1939 that Hitler got his wish. That day my father got me out of bed at dawn, "Come, let's take a walk". We walked to a chapel behind which there was a bench under a large tree with an amazing view over the city of Fulda and the majestic Wasserkuppe Mountain. We were silent as dawn was coming up. Then my father broke the silence, sadness filling his eyes: "This morning at 5am the Austrian corporal attacked Poland. France and England, who have a treaty of mutual aid in case of aggression, will have to declare war on us. This Austrian corporal who fancies himself a military genius will drown our country in fire and blood." A mixture of excitement and anxiety gripped my throat watching my father, eyes to the sky, holding back tears. Were his thoughts with his eldest son already on the Western front? "I hope the Americans will soon come into the war to support France and England. They alone are able to put the

Austrian corporal in his place. US power has no limit. Come, let's go to the chapel to pray for us all."

In September 1940, my brother Josef came home on leave. He told us about his campaign in France that had taken him from Le Havre and crossing Brittany without firing a shot all the way to Brest. There, finally, they met with resistance from some fortifications. Their opponents, without support from the Navy that had already parted the French garrison, had quickly thrown in the towel. For us the result was pure pleasure: the beach, the sun, the good life. He brought gifts for the whole family. He found the French very hospitable but not happy to be paid in French francs - they wanted our much coveted Reichsmarks (in these early stages of the war the German soldiers were ordered to use only the local currency).

My father was given permission to hire three French prisoners to help in his production of leather gear for the German army. It would be a welcome addition because it was difficult to find German workers - most of them were either soldiers or in armament work. My father did not lack work, thanks in part to Mr. Hirsch, who continued to supply him with otherwise scarce raw materials. French prisoners turned out to be good workers and, indeed, my father could pay off Hirsch quickly enough. He came once a month to spend the evening with us when the French had finished their day and he often remained to dine with us. With the new motorway, Kassel-Frankfurt, the trip only took him an hour and a half. Police checks increased even on secondary roads. "To this day I have never had a problem", he said, "but I will never be without my military certificate of my rank as colonel in the German army and my Cross of Merit." The last time he came to us was just before Christmas 1941. He brought gifts, cigars for my father and real coffee for my mother. We thought he must have good relations with the authorities of Kassel but eventually it was not enough to save his life.

*

The two hundred French prisoners of the region were housed in the former village hall and worked in the surrounding farms. Their life was not particularly hard. They were supervised by a former officer of WWI and two or three soldiers from the same generation, not by fanatics. As their sleeping quarters were a few miles away, the prisoners who worked for us were allowed to spend the whole work week with us. There was no report of any prisoner trying to escape - their life here was not bad at that time.

Most of the prisoners were doing farm work, filling in for the farmers that were away at war. Those who worked with my father seemed in no hurry to leave us. Sometimes they replaced my mother in the kitchen, time for French cuisine. On Saturday afternoon they were scouring the countryside in search of snails or frogs. They surprised us with garlic dishes and other ingredients unfamiliar to us. They asked their families to send gifts through the military mail and even received wine. As a result, on Sunday mornings the kitchen was very busy with six to eight prisoners joining us for lunch with their guards.

Some meals were extraordinary, especially when my Mother had found some beef. As for my father, he shared his bottle of schnapps from of his stash. My mother was thrilled with real coffee, supplied by the French. For a long time in Germany, there had been nothing but the tasteless "ersatzkaffee" (artificial coffee made from roasted barley spiced with chicory). She would serve their good coffee along with a fruit tart. For the French prisoners, it was not a bad life, at least they were away from the war.

One of these fellows caused us serious trouble with the Gestapo. Not suspecting anything, my father gave him a radio brought from France by Josef. Father had not realized that the man had listened to Radio London and that he boasted about it to his comrades. Among these prisoners were also communists, fascists, and one with contacts with the French resistance. The French police forwarded their report to their office in Frankfurt, as well as to the Gestapo. A commando of four police men came to investigate. One of the prisoners had informed them that a

German employer had a radio and one of the prisoners had used it to listen to Radio London. After this prisoner had suffered severe interrogation, they were trying to make him say that his German employer was complicit but he did not say anything. The camp guards were arrested and replaced by the German police. My father was deprived of 'prisoner-employees.' He ended up destroying the French radio.

From that time on, the threat of a visit from the Gestapo was always hanging over the life of our whole family.

*

After my induction into the National Work Service I arrived at the barracks in Glauchau with all these images in mind. It was my turn to become a part of the military system of the regime. First endless forms and questionnaires and lots of paperwork. Nothing was done without proper recording in true German fashion. After that we were led to the canteen for lunch and then to a gathering in the courtyard. First there was roll call. The Land Hessen-Süd was well represented among the young recruits. The officers were presented to us: the Adjutant Administrative officer, the Quartermaster, our Company Commander and the NCOs, the, Section Heads and Group Leaders. We were the last, those of the 1924 class, which would be going into the RAD rather than directly into the military. We were dismissed to our rooms, one for six soldiers. Bunk beds, one locker each. After a meager dinner, we had some free time to get to know our fellow recruits. Some were from my home town, Huenfeld, and some from the surrounding area. Naturally, we young people tended to associate according to their places of origin.

Next morning we change our clothes: dress for the first time in the uniform of the RAD, the National Work Force, complete with the official tool of this national service: a spade. We were told that this spade was not only our main work tool but also the 'insignia' of the service we were to render to our country.' It had to be polished to a silver brilliance each morning. We had to learn to 'present it' just as if it were a weapon.

At seven in the evening, the sirens called us to the parade grounds for the 'Oath of Faithful Service' to the light of a hundred torches. We were divided into sections of twenty recruits each. Our section commander was a brute with a mean demeanor, inspiring immediate dislike. We were four from Huenefeld. To my right, a guy from the far away province of Pommern who spoke Polish better than German, and knew a bit of Russian also. We went forward to the oath ceremony. Our battalion commander entered the court flanked by his adjutant. He climbed on a podium and hoisted the Nazi colors. "Present arms"! We present our gleaming spade. Then the battalion commander shouts:

"Repeat after me: I swear to be faithful to our Führer Adolf Hitler and to obey the orders of our Leaders."

My Pomeranian neighbor mumbled under his breath. Me too. I thought of my father.

Before leaving, he had taken me aside: "My son, even if you do not go to the front, you'll have to swear loyalty to that Austrian corporal and everything else. Do as the others, but at the same time think that there is nothing more important in life than the respect of the Ten Commandments that the Church taught you. You will do everything to save yourself and your companions and you will never forget, whatever happens, what your parents expect of you". The way he held me in his arms made it clear to me that he did not believe the six months of RAD service would be all I was to face. He was right.

Conclusion of the ceremony: patriotic songs, the "Deutschland Über Alles" and the "Horst Wessel Lied", the anthem of the Nazi Party that we knew too well. Since 1933 it was obligatory singing by all school children at every opportunity without any explanation. In reality we were not sure at all what we were singing and it was only some years later that I got to understand the macabre meaning of words.

How many of us took that oath without believing and sang without understanding? Impossible to know, we had no time to think. Already new rules: in two days we would begin basic military training. We would be given another uniform and we would get a gun. Farewell spade! We were instructed to only wear the uniform in town. Is that clear?

Our section chief joined us in the canteen and sat at our table. Basically, he wants to get to know us. It is an interrogation meal. He takes notes about us and begins with a young man of Marburg. Name, date of birth. Family environment? Studies? The guy got his bachelor's degree with excellent grades. His father was a professor at the University of the same city. Not a chance - not only did the section chief not congratulate him but his face shows the most obvious contempt. Surely, this is one of those illiterates pleased that circumstances allow him to exert power over educated people.

Nazism had guys like that arise from nowhere, starting through the SA gangs who had spread terror. They were recruited from day workers who had lost their jobs, from former communists and many others who lost their social standing as a result of the devastating German depression. Because the Party was presented as "anti-capitalist" it had never lost an opportunity to attack the intellectuals as "decadent" and far from the people. The regime could boast of having been able to give work to six million unemployed, offer two weeks of paid vacation and an opportunity for social advancement, but only for supporters of their regime. A strange group of individuals were put into unexpected positions replacing people of value who were being systematically arrested.

I remembered the example of our neighbor, Alfred Habersack, a very active social democrat who never stopped opposing the takeover of the Nazis in our region. My father told him to be cautious and to think of his wife and daughters. In September 1934, the Gestapo arrested and imprisoned him in the Buchenwald concentration camp. He was a 35 year vigorous masonry worker. Two years later, he was a toothless old man who had returned with a torn ear, a lifeless look, unable to resume any work activity. He committed suicide soon after.

The same happened with one my father's cousins, who was a pastor of a nearby parish. He preached against the terror of the regime. A Nazi in uniform attended the service. The next day at dawn, the Gestapo came to get the courageous priest. No luggage, pants or shirt will be necessary, the police had told him. Six months later, a simple post card had informed my father that his cousin had died in prison. He was also at Buchenwald.

Now back to my induction time. I had no trouble imagining our section chief beating any opponent of Nazism. "Hey! You Polack, you know how to speak German?" he shouted at my neighbor, the guy from Pomerania. Johann simply replied that he was an ethnic German born in Poland. He had little schooling having to help his parents on the farm.

When my turn comes I hesitantingly say I got an accounting degree and that I was a bank clerk before being summoned to the RAD. I could have told him many more things if I had not had to deal with this kind of dick-head.

*

I always liked to study. My mother taught me to read, write, and count when I was 5 years old. She saw that I had a great thirst for knowledge. In primary school my first grade report card was excellent. After an interview with the principal, Willy Unverzagt, my father decided to get involved in my education early and explained the meaning of getting ahead to me.

In 1938 this same principal had tried to enroll me in high school in Fulda. I was rejected, identified as the son of anti-Nazi. Willy Unverzagt was sorry, but he had thought about plan B. He remembered that I had shown a knack for selling.

Realizing the practical difficulties for my parents to support me, I had an idea. I went to get the permission of the pastor of our parish to allow me to sell the weekly Catholic 'City of God' magazine. This magazine was sold only by annual subscription and not a single subscription had been placed in his parish. If I could succeed to sell subscriptions the priest promised me a 20% commission. My parents did not believe I could do it - this subscription seemed too expensive but I had thought about a plan of action."Let me do it. All I need is your bike, Dad."

The next day I took action. Willy Unverzagt was the first one where I could test my sales approach. At the end of my presentation, he said with a sly smile: "My dear Aloysius, you'll sell your magazine because you know how to convince people!"He was my first customer.

With his help, I drew up a list of potentials that could be approached, and those who were genuinely Nazis. At the end of the day, I sold six subscriptions. It was exciting!

The day after I tackled some officials who had not yet been forced to join the Nazi Party. To spend as much as 60 Reichsmarks for a subscription was a severe handicap. Then I had the idea to soften this resistance by asking their wives to attend the presentation of the magazine - they were always the weak link. Because of them the husband listened to me and I could talk about faith, even though many wanted to do without God. I continued my talk by saying that it was always better to stay on good terms with Him because no one is entirely master of his destiny and the end for each of us could happen more quickly than previously thought, especially being at war. Five Reichsmarks per month really was a small price to pay for a charitable act toward God and his Church. My order book began to fill. Usually, I succeeded in getting the subscription. If not, I pretended to take leave on these words: "May God protect you and forgive you." Many times, I stayed a little longer with the wife and often she then wanted to talk to her husband. Success was in the pocket. The second day, I had sold eight subscriptions.

One of those sales was special. He was a tailor whose business was booming. He was a member of the Nazi Party and the only one to wear the SS uniform that he proudly exhibited in his shop. My father knew him well. He was the same age as my sister Catherina. Appointments made, I arrive at their home. His wife is there. I immediately get to the point. The answer came quickly: a definite no. Without letting it put me off I continued: "Hermann, three years ago you went every Sunday to Mass with your wife and two daughters. After that you spent time at the pub to drink schnapps and a beer with friends. It was a pleasant and friendly time. Then Nazi propaganda influenced a number of good Catholics who changed their colors, either because it was profitable or to parade their uniform in the streets and greet others with a Heil Hitler! You're the one wearing the black uniform of the SS. Your wife and daughters continue to go every Sunday to church. For you "religion is the opium of the people. With only one suit you make, you earn more money than a year's subscription to the 'Stadt Gottes'. You know that the war will soon break out. Like you, I may have to go to war. I know I will come back, because I believe in God and I know God is with me. You have forsaken the religion, that is your right. I thought by selling you the magazine you would stay in touch with God. Believe me, the day will come when you implore Him to give you His grace. I hope that He will forgive you then."

With that, I packed up my things and turned around. The reaction was not long in coming, the tailor's wife caught up with me for a subscription. As for Hermann, the only thing that interested him was that, above all, that I will tell no one! After six weeks, I had sold 72 subscriptions and gave my mother my earnings of 864 Reichsmarks, a good amount of money at that time.

This is probably why Willy Unverzagt thought the place for me should be at the Fulda business school. He knew its director, Mr. Schlitzer. My father agreed but the price of tuition for a year was too high. No problem! You pay for six months and complete the whole year's program in six months! My father could not hide his skepticism without trying to discourage me.

A week later, my mother and I took the train to Fulda. I had to fight hard with the school principal to get him to accept our proposal. I had to talk him into making an exception, I wanted so much to be enrolled!

It was good to study in Fulda, in a city 100% Catholic, without any enthusiasm for the Nazis. When the Nazis wanted to appoint a new County Party Chief they had to get someone from elsewhere to come to Kassel to accept this Nazi party position. There was no one to be found in Fulda to take this job!

In the Schlitzer Business School, still being a private institution, classes began with prayer, in contrast to the state schools. We formed a rather special class made up of students of families hostile to the regime. The school had a good atmosphere of fair competition. At noon each got out his sandwich for a lunch break of half an hour. In the evening I took the train back to Hünfeld where my sister Clara lived but I spent the weekend with my parents.

At the end of my six months I left Schlitzer with a Certificate of Studies in retail, wholesale and industry, with an accounting specialty. With my father I went to the local Raiffeisen Bank to get a three-year apprenticeship. I was 16. What a joy to start my professional life, although materially it did not represent much. I gave my modest salary to my mother who gave me a small part as 'pocket money'.

*

Back to my induction into the Service: I was not going to tell any of this to my section chief. I simply said that I had worked with my parents at the end of primary school. "Too bad that you were born December 9, 1924, because if your father had jerked off instead of knock up your mother, you'd probably have been born in January 1925 and the service to the Eastern Front wouldn't be for you!" I was appalled by the crudeness of his language. What is he thinking? Should I laugh at such despicable bad humor? Above all, watch it, so that he could not see all the disgust I felt for him because I knew I would pay dearly if he found out. I could not wait to get away from the table.

In the following days, there was all military training with weapons, rifles, machine guns and pistols like a normal military service. The strongest got special training in heavy machine guns, twelve hours of daily training. I didn't mind. Since the age of ten, sports were a great part of our lives. The large sports field next to the school was never empty! Boys and girls did the same exercises: long jump and height, speed race, long distance running, even a thousand yards. At age 12, I was in great shape, beginning to look at the girls. Some already were real little women - exercise showed its good results. My mother had discovered traces of my first wet dream when making my bed. I had a heart-to-heart talk with my father who was pleased: you will be a true man, filling me with pride.

Anyway, we were prepared for this early military life. At ages between 10 and 14 years we were automatically inducted into the 'Jungvolk'. We wore a uniform but without insignia. In our area we were not subject to Nazi indoctrination. It looked a bit like the organization of the Boy Scouts. In the evening we walked and we gathered around the fire to sing, tell stories and we returned home before 10pm. At age 12, my classmates elected me leader of our group, which meant organizing games in the forest, war games, of course, between Comanches and Apaches.

Regardless of the circumstances, thought should always precede the decision - that was what I was learning from my comrades. It was as early as 1939 when I had acquired a taste for physical prowess along with a strong liking for personal achievement.

At the Glauchau barracks we soon settled into a routine. On Sundays, after lunch, we had free time to go out. Small groups were formed, often the same three good friends. We went to one of the dance cafés of the city. An orchestra played and dance partners were not lacking, many young women already were 'war widows' in search of adventure. No need to deploy all the tricks of the great seducer to find a partner, just do some laps on the dance floor and take home a date for a nightcap that very often turned into a small meal usually made of fried potatoes. Hence an expression that circulated among soldiers to give a name to this kind of adventure: 'Ein Bratkartoffelverhältnis' (literally a 'fried-potato relationship'). In 1942, it was no longer easy to get food. Even with our ration tickets the grocer often had very little to offer.

We were young and we did not care much about the future.

*

Chapter 2

Getting to Know a Little about Russia

In early May we were called to the courtyard. "From here on out you no longer are permitted to call or write to anyone. This is a security issue. We leave in two days for the Eastern front."

On May 10, 1942, we left our barracks very early, and climbed into trucks for the railroad station. We took the compartments reserved for the troops and put our gear on the platforms. Goodbye Germany!

As we crossed the border into Poland the train was rearranged to include four well-armed platform cars and many more cars for soldiers. Johann, the Pomeranian, was detached to man a heavy machine gun on one of the air defense platform cars.

We were given instructions on how to react to an attack of the Polish resistance and to an air attack. These drills did not detract us from admiring the beauty of the land we crossed, in the full glory of the arrival of spring, but I was surprised by the otherwise featureless landscape. The villages with their tiny churches seemed very miserable.

We crossed into Russia. Evening fell, the train stops. It seems that we will be in Kursk next morning. We had the usual everyday meal, a bowl of soup, bread and water, while two sections stood guard on either side of our convoy. Around midnight, the train departed at very low speeds. We pull into a station and are stopped on a side track. Soldiers everywhere. Five hundred yards to the right, I see a column of tanks, under camouflage nets below the trees. Suddenly, there is a roar of explosions from the station. We rush to our guns in the cars, as we were taught to do earlier the same afternoon. Section chiefs screaming: "Spitfire attack! Spitfire attack!" The planes scream even louder dropping their bombs while their machine guns spit tracer bullets into the night. A torrent of steel, chaos all over, a feeling that we are all done for. Blessed Virgin, protect us!

Emerging from nowhere, our own fighters join in, they counter attack, harass the Spitfires and manage to take over the sky. It's finished. It only remains for us to measure the extent of damage and count our dead. Our battalion has lost twelve men and there are twenty-two wounded, including two of our gunners. Johann the Pomeranian is alive! Two trucks burned. No more need for drills to prepare us for action! Our bloody "baptism of fire" had just taken place.

*

After the Spitfire attack, we moved on, no more dallying. Our convoy departed southbound to a small railway station, about 60 kilometers from Kursk. Our new 'garrison' is a former collective farm consisting of simple huts for families of the farm workers. Everything is in a state of disrepair. Two weeks of intensive work make them into a habitable space.

Are we going to be here to fight the war or for the work we were drafted to do? Our first task ahead is to prepare the ground for the construction of an air strip that would receive a squadron of Messerschmitt fighter-bombers called 'Fighter Squadron Freiherr von Richthofen'.

This was hard manual work that got us down quickly. I was thinking about how to get out of it. Even at 17 I always tried to distinguish myself, but not by obediently following the herd. I thought that I could make a better contribution to my duties than by this hard manual labor. There were plenty of much stronger guys for this work with greater skills as masons, earth workers and carpenters. Clearly, my skills were elsewhere. I was searching for a better way for me.

Was it the fact of being thrown into working on an airfield, something in the context of aviation? I thought back to a 1936 episode back home when a single-engine aircraft with two pilots and six passengers onboard crash-landed in a potato field not far from my home. We all ran like mad to see what kind of flying monster that was. I never had the opportunity to be close to a plane. This chance event aroused a passion for aviation in me which our friend Willy Unverzagt fueled by lending me books on the history of flight. From there my dream of building my own plane was born.

It was a project not far from being foolish but somehow I had the gift of convincing those around me, starting with my father. He promised to take me to see some people that could provide me with materials and assistance. I had gone to work, spending hours after school to complete plans and to raise technical issues, submitting them to the principal who began to doubt my judgement in such a complicated matter. Perhaps I also had the gift of taking adults back into the dreams of their own childhood. Willy Unverzagt bought fully into my story and he wanted to interest the local press, perhaps to see if I would give up once confronted with the harsh light of publicity. Instead it just strengthened my determination. I was going to create something they have never seen!

At last the day of glory arrived! It was sunny, the wind blew from the south facing my make shift runway. There are many onlookers, my father hardly able to conceal his concern while Unverzagt was conversing with three journalists and the photographer. We saw our family doctor, with his emergency kit. All of the people who had helped me were there.

Gathering all my courage, I spoke to all the world about my idea and thanked those who trusted in me and had helped, not forgetting to add: "Say a prayer that everything goes well and that I will make it without too much damage." With that, I climbed into my rickety 'flying machine' held level by my friends. My motor bike that was to tow my aircraft had started. Going downhill and with good headwind, my flight was quickly taking off and the tow rope had separated as planned. I was aloft at an altitude of about twenty meters when suddenly a strong gust made my glider veer to the right and I crash landed some thirty meters below. I came out of it with some injuries and with immense pride to have met this challenge. The next day we read in the local press: "An unprecedented feat." I was not even 16 years old. Yes, I had created an event by doing something that no one asked me to do and it was going through the press.

So, if I wanted to get out from under the onerous excavation work, I had to offer something that no one asked for and that no one had thought of. I had noticed that there was no record of the everyday life of us workers, more than six hundred soldiers and RAD men. What a pity! No one kept track of this and the public back home knows nothing about our toils! Why not do stories about it for them?

I decided to put this idea to the man in charge, Neubauer, head of general administration of our group. I proposed that the subject of my first edition would be about the site of the future airport, about the significance of the work, with a series of interviews with men from different regions of our country to make people back home proud of their hard working sons. I would take photos of them for their parents. Without waiting for Neubauer's response I went to work, using my little box camera. The next day, my first article was on Neubauer's table.

An hour later in his office, I find him waiting for me with the battalion commander who did not look comfortable behind his heavy glasses. "What makes you think you could do this? Did you study journalism?"

I invited him to look at the reports about me from the section chief. Slightly annoyed, he retorts that these reports are useless but he liked it that I did not 'beat around the bush' answering his questions. I told him every person has his qualities and it appears the best way for me to serve our unit is to ensure that every soldier maintains a link with his native region thanks to my articles. The colonel thanked me and left the office. My article and photographs received his approval.

The next day, the Work Group Leader announced that I am officially named 'war reporter' and he handed me a special card stating my new position. First step: the battalion tailor sewed on the sleeves of my uniform an armband stating my new role. I am no longer part of Section 2 but attached to the administrative department of Neubauer. Comrades in my area come and congratulate me calling me a special reporter for the Fuldaer newspaper.

Our reporting service proved very effective. I issued articles specialized for each region back home. Under military rules, my stories did not accurately locate our battalion. I just describe our work to be in close liaison with a unit of army engineers, saying that we were working at the 'highway to the Volga', meant to facilitate the transport of troops to the front.

My typewriter and my little camera had rescued me from the pick and shovel! I was determined to do more of this.

Meanwhile, the work of the airport for our fighter-bombers was well advanced. The advance air men groups, maintenance men and administration staff were already there, housed in two operations barracks. Things went well between me and these men. My position as war reporter opened all doors for me. I learned that two of the mess halls were to be equipped to serve future officers and NCOs. How would they find enough building materials to furnish these bare places? I told them that I would come back the day after with the answers. Back from the aviators, I told Neubauer about this problem.

"You? How could you get extra supplies for the mess hall?"

"Trust me, I will take care of everything."
As a first step I asked permission to visit the nearby collective farm to see if there was something there to write about.

"Okay, Johann can accompany you - he speaks enough Russian. You will take a cart and two horses. Johann has a machine gun and a pistol, but you will not be armed with anything other than your camera."

Off we went to explore the Kolkhoz, five miles away. On the way we saw several improvised graves of fallen German soldiers, probably ambushed. Suddenly gunfire erupts, we are caught in a crossfire with bullets flying left and right! Johann hands me the reins of the horses, I was praying to the Virgin Mary to protect us when heavy machine guns and cannons scare away the partisans. Close call! Less than ten minutes later, two German armored cars come our way. An officer asks us to show our papers:

"What are you doing in this rotten corner?"

"Lieutenant, I am a war journalist, we are on the way to the collective farm located one kilometer further down the road. I am writing a report to our men's regional press at home so our comrades keep in touch with their families in Germany."

"That's all well and good but here we are in a war zone and the Soviets want to know about our preparations for our next big offensive. Since you are going to the Kolkhoz, tell the manager there to stop these partisan attacks or will I reduce everything to dust."

Ten Minutes later we stop in front of the main house of the Kolkhoz. A crowd gathers, at once a man comes to us. I tell them I'm a journalist, I would like to do a story on the life of a Kolkhoz. Johann is about to translate but the man already welcomes me in German before telling onlookers what is happening.

The head of the collective farm takes us on a tour of the place telling us the history of the agricultural cooperative. He takes out various documents and, like a guide in a museum, shows the photos that decorate his office. Can I take pictures, too? Certainly, and we do it right under the portrait of Stalin. This was clever. If this picture fell into the hands of a Soviet commissar it would show his bravery and patriotism in the presence of an enemy!

I wanted to put the record straight: We are here not as enemies, all we want is to establish a relationship of trust. "Tell your friends to stop attacking German units that move on this road. Our commanders know your influence over your followers and you risk serious reprisals". The man tried to measure me and then he said," I'll do everything I can to prevent a massacre."

A crowd had gathered in the courtyard. A kind of buffet had been prepared: bread, butter, vodka. Like all leaders, our new friend went there for a little speech in Russian, Johann translating for me. As expected, people applauded at the end, and we approached the table, taking a photo here, a photo there. Then, a glass of vodka in hand, a toast in Russian and emptying his glass. I thought I should do the same. My God! This vodka was like liquid fire, at least 80 proof! The collective farmers were laughing at me being out of breath! Butter sandwiches extinguished the fire. I could resume my journalistic work: pictures of villagers, houses, farm animals.

The Chief wanted to know when I would return. "As soon as possible." He told me reassuringly: "There will be no more attacks on the road." Then he handed me two bottles of vodka and proposed a deal: "If you can get salt for me, I can give you butter. We are short of salt, even for bread, we have none left." It can be done, because now we are friends." To seal this statement, he kisses me on the mouth! Wow!

Friends won among enemies! Good job! We traded our salt for their butter. "I will write my report and you, Johann, take care of the horses. OK"?

At the camp, two letters were waiting. My parents and my brother Josef had written to me. The latter told me that he had three days leave to visit me in Kursk and he gave me his company's phone number. My relationship with Neubauer made things easier. Communication is quickly established. I came across a friend of my brother who tells me that the Red Army tried to encircle Minsk and the infantry division of my brother launched a counteroffensive supported by artillery and airplanes. "If I have more news, I'll call you immediately." The line was cut.

I had not seen my brother since 1941 before leaving for Poland. I knew he took part in the offensive against the Red Army in the center of the front. There was no contact with his division. "Wait for the leader of Josef Pappert's section to contact you".'No news, good news', a proverb good in peace, but when war rages ... Ten days later, a letter from my parents informed me that my brother was seriously injured and was in a military hospital awaiting his repatriation. His division had indeed participated in the pursuit of the Russians. They had advanced so quickly that the firing of their own artillery that was to support them had hit them instead! In spite of his foot injury, Josef had hoisted a comrade on his back to put him out of reach of the 'friendly fire' before collapsing himself. For my brother, the war was over!

Until he had tasted my Kolkhoz butter the chef did not believe it: "Son of a dog! This is real butter! Man oh man, do not tell anyone, not even Neubauer!"

- May I still make a sandwich?

- Yes, but hurry, the boss arrives in my kitchen any time now.

I was in my office writing my next article: 'Salt for Butter' when the Work Group leader and the Staff Major enter with an air of conspirators, closing the door behind them. "Butter is scarce for us, even in Germany. We need to think about the best use we can make of it. Where are you with the project about building the officers' mess hall?"

- I'll know more tomorrow after returning from the Airport project.

- Perfect. See you tomorrow".

Today, three letters in my mail locker. My sisters Clara and Catherina gave me some news of their families. Both got married, but this was not easy because the grip of the Nazi regime on everybody's life cut into in every detail of privacy. The marriage of my sisters was a perfect illustration. Although engaged, the agreement of the families was far from sufficient. To publish the banns they had to present City Hall with a number of certificates to prove that parents, grandparents and great-grandparents were 'pure race' and that we had no Jewish ancestors. It took months and the engaged had to be patient.

The second letter was from my parents, previously opened by censors. The correspondence of my father was monitored. The third came from Glauchau. It was by the hand of my last 'fried potatoes relationship'. The young war widow sent a letter full of emotions of the memory of our three evenings. She had found a buyer for her house and she left for the United States to find his parents. "Maybe we'll see each other after the war? I'll send you my address in America."

I continued to visit our airmen crews who were full of admiration for the work of our battalion. No Messerschmitts yet in sight but the runway was already operational, as well as the impeccably appointed barracks for the staff and the shelters for aircraft.

The head of the officers' mess was about thirty years old. There was an immediate rapport between us. In civilian life, he had worked in catering. I told him about my intention to organize an officers mess at home, except that I lacked the experience. Could I go with him the next time he will go to stock up supplies? "With pleasure, we will go together for our first major supply trip today because the planes arrive after tomorrow."

*

On these trips I met a 30 year old Austrian. Three years earlier, he had volunteered in the Air Force, responsible for maintenance of aircraft and test flying on occasion. To listen to him, Austria, and especially Vienna, was a paradise before the occupation by the German army. "Occupation? A strange word. I thought that in Austria, Hitler was welcomed as a hero, a liberator! I had heard the enthusiasm of the population on the radio. In addition, he is Austrian!" Heavy silence.

We drive without exchanging a word then, suddenly: "War broke out three years ago. Mussolini and his parody of an army will soon be wiped off the map. The Japanese attacking America have awakened a superpower that will destroy them. Perhaps it will last long, but what is certain is that in the end Japan will no longer be a military power, just like Germany. The Allies already landed in Morocco and soon they will be in Europe. Do you still believe in a German victory?" Such remarks touched my heart, but I thought it more prudent to hide my feelings. "You know, you are 30 and I am only 17, and I have been in Russia for only three months, my knowledge of war is limited." Again, silence. Then the Austrian turned to me:

- Can I trust you?
- If it's a question of honor, yes.

He finally spilled the beans: "I am a communist like my father. I studied medicine. I was 26 when he told me: learn mechanics, because soon you will have to go to military service. I have a friend who will train you, he will deliver a mechanic certificate to you and, with this in hand, you will volunteer for the air force. It may keep you out of combat. I have prepared everything." All the family and relations of the man were communists. After the "Anschluss" forced by the Nazis in Austria, his family had destroyed all documents likely to betray their political activities. Fortunately, the Nazis, beginning with the SS, were so obsessed with the Jews that the Communists had been largely left alone for a while. By the way, my companion explained the origin of the Nazi anthem to me, the "Horst Wessel Lied". Horst Wessel, a young rogue member of S.A died 1930 in a clash with the Communists. The S.A. had made him a martyr through this song that left no doubt about their intentions: Death to the Communists, and to any conservative and traditional values.

My turn to make a confession: "I am Catholic and my father is an important member of the Catholic Centre Party, and therefor he is in trouble." "Then you are not in favor of the Nazis?" Assured of my sincerity he drew from his pocket a condensed version of Marx's 'Das Kapital'. "Hide it under your uniform and read it tonight. Tomorrow when you pass through the airport you can return it to me discreetly, without comment. I'll introduce our chef. For the rest we'll talk later."

Like every night, I went to give my report to Neubauer. I gave him my plan to go to the army supply depot and told him of the appointment with the cook of the officers' mess. "My word but you move real fast!" Maybe, but I was exhausted to the point of asking the special favor to take my meals in the office so I could complete today's article which I wanted send in very early, before leaving.

Then I went to bed to read my Karl Marx! I read and read. It was exciting. My head was spinning, an excitement came over me. "Workers of the world unite!" Liberty, Equality Fraternity!

How can we believe in equality when everything clearly shows that everyone is different? When each follows his own way, different from his neighbor. This huge country is called the Soviet Union, and its abominable application of the doctrine of Marx and Engels! I imagined a news story. The next morning, I saw my Communist driver at the airport and gave him back his book quietly. He watched for a reaction from me. I simply said: "This is amazing. Careful."

*

The mess chef's name was Anton. He was the sergeant in charge of organizing the entire food supply. "If you want, I'm leaving in an hour and you can come with me." He was to fill one truck with food but we were going with two trucks. "Why two?" "Wait and see," replied Anton.

At the entrance of the supply deposit, one truck was left outside, out of sight. We entered the compound with one truck and we went to check in around 11am. He showed our documents and started to load the vehicle. At noon, we left the supply depot through the gate and got properly checked out. We then waited out of sight until we saw the check point team being relieved for their lunch hour. We then got the second truck and reentered the depot showing the new guard the same documents as the first time as if nothing had happened, loaded the second truck with the same cargo and left before the original guard team had returned from lunch. Two trucks full of food double rations without a trace!

Back at camp I file my report to a very pensive Neubauer who meditates as he listens to me. My stomach is growling - it's already 4 hours in the afternoon! The canteen is deserted but the chef serves me good things with the bonus of a bottle of beer. Why this treatment? "On orders from Neubauer." My 17 years begin to impress my big boss ...

It was early June 1942 and time went fast between my war journalist work and organizer of all kinds, the days chasing each other. Between Kolkhoz and operation 'Salt for Butter', reports and photos ... my sleeping hours were reduced to a few, and I had almost no time to spend with my fellow Fuldaens.

I had to think hard about how to equip the officers mess hall. I collected a few crafts men from the airstrip construction team and with these men in tow we went to see the barracks that was to house the future Luftwaffe mess so they can learn about its layout. This way they could begin to plan their work and somehow find the necessary building materials.

In the meantime, Johann and I made another visit to the Kolkhoz with two bags of salt in our carriage. Three casks of butter are ready for us. Personally, I would have done without the obligatory vodka ritual by to no avail. I took advantage of everybody's festive mood to take some more pictures.

Another idea came to me because I had noticed the strong personal interest by my superiors in that Russian butter. Alone with my boss, I made a proposal:

"For you and the Works Leader, I can arrange an air shipment of butter to your homes."

An hour later, I was in the colonel's office. He and Neubauer were interested in my somewhat dangerous proposal. "Just give me your home address and butter will arrive there for your families." What about shipping?" Just let me do it, OK!

- One more thing: tomorrow you will have my article on 'Salt for Butter '.

On my project to use our men to build up the airmen's mess hall Neubauer merely gave me a 'Do as usual.' I always created the impression of requesting his authorization simply to keep my superiors informed of my initiatives.

He then said: "To show you how much confidence we have in your activities, we have made a car and a driver available to you."

WOW! It was a French car, a Renault. My driver was armed, while as a 'War Reporter' I was protected only by my faith and my determination to move forward. Guess which one was better protected?

At the airstrip I quickly found Anton and offered him a ride to see the progress of the mess construction. The efficiency of our men was impressive. I had given preference to men from my home area, from Huenfeld and Fulda. It gave this project an additional element of caring. They were thrilled to have been taken off the back breaking earth moving work for an indoor job where they could use their professional expertise. They were working fast: storage bins for the bombs and ammunition were already operational and so were the platforms for the air defense batteries. The first planes were announced to arrive the following day. Trucks loaded with bombs were to precede them in the morning.

Looking for my friends from Fulda and Hünfeld, I find them at the end of the track, working with the latest defenses. With eyes wide open and laughing, my good friends see me step out of my car complete with my driver and a noncommissioned officer. "The car, it's yours?" says a friend from Hünfeld, with a smirk. With the innocent bravado of youth, I answered affirmatively, "Yes, it is mine for now. Now, to work! Group all of you here, we'll take a picture." I formed two groups and took two shots with the airstrip in the background, but showing it as if it were just a piece of highway to make sure the censors would let it pass. Then I wrote down the name of each soldier, for their relatives back in Hünfeld and Fulda. "Next time I come by plane!" Laughing loud they sent me on my way.

Returning to the mess, I took pictures of the new interior, the bar stocked with spirits, fine wines, and tables for four guests or more. Anton told me that tomorrow, if everything went as planned, the first planes would be here and a welcome party will be organized. "If you want to come with some of your men, we will receive you with great pleasure." An invitation of this kind cannot be refused, I will come with my two superiors.

I immediately developed the photos that I hoped would serve to inspire our carpenters. I passed on the invitation of the airmen to Neubauer who invited me to dinner with the Works Leader. What a meal, complete with two bottles of white Moselle wines, an excellent epilogue of a very busy day.

I had to think of everything about the opening of our own mess. Time was short. First objective: the supply. The best would be to go to the supply depot, again with two trucks. I would personally choose our drivers, especially the one who would accompany me. Meanwhile, the head chef would make his list. Before this official resupply, I would have to make a stop at the Kolkhoz to get some news and continue with the 'salt for butter' operation. Neubauer, stunned by this ambitious schedule, declared himself convinced: "It's good everything is clear, follow your program, but do not forget our appointment this evening with the airmen."

We arrived in the Work Leader's car. The mess hall was already full. The room echoed with laughter, the clinking of glasses and the good mood. Anton slips a word in the ear of an officer who asks for a moment of silence so we can introduce ourselves and thank my superiors for the excellent work done by our men of the RAD. Thunderous applause. My leaders took their seats at the table with the General Staff of the Luftwaffe and the Company

Commander of the Army Engineers. As for me, I have plenty of time to observe the performance of the service: Anton oversees the bar with a bartender. Two other servers are busy indoors. I asked Anton if I can take some photos for an article in the army press. No problem.

The evening takes its course, group by group, in a relaxed atmosphere with good discussions and jokes. Look! An officer wearing a cross on his uniform. It is the chaplain of the squadron who is also a medic. Together, we leave the mess and he shows me a building used as a field hospital and where, on Sundays, he held Mass. He has no objection if we join the airmen. Upon returning I discussed the matter with my superiors. After a long silence, the Works Leader simply agreed for those of RAD who want to attend Mass: "Know that this is contrary to the spirit of the National Socialist Party. Tell yourself that you will be considered responsible." Message received. It is a thinly veiled warning. It is time for me to do the shipment of liquefied butter. It would make them complicit and thus unlikely to denounce me.

And the war we were in? It was coming to us, slowly but surely, ready to throw us into its horrors, already providing the background to our lives: all night the parade of motorized vehicles, the uninterrupted passage of Panzers and an armada of other vehicles moving to the front. The last Messerschmitts arrived with their supreme commander, a Colonel of the Air Force, awarded the highest distinction. His plane was adorned with fifty-six Iron Cross telling about as many downed planes. Briefed by Anton I rushed to the airport to take a picture of this air combat ace standing next to his plane. This picture naturally found a place in the stories on my comrades from Hünfeld and Fulda.

Back to the supply depot with my two trucks. The drivers knew the Anton method. The actual loading of the trucks, one by one, made some of us very nervous. The NCO control officer was worried: "I think it will soon blow up on us. Our supply room is filled to the brim. It seems that we must be prepared to supply two armies for a great offensive. Thanks for the tip."

I pretended to have forgotten a few items. "No problem, add them." With the second driver to the 'spirits, tobacco and other comfort products' department, just doubling the authorized amount. On leaving, the control team had changed, as expected. New chat on the war, on my journalist activity, taking photos and this and that, until the drivers show their impatience, honking.

- It's good! Let's go!

We left the depot with our official documents in perfect order, no evidence of any wrong doing.

"Our mess is stocked for a long time!" Good news to put in my report to Neubauer. Of course, mine is not strictly speaking a 'report', it was more like a discussion, a mutual exchange of information. My relationships with my supervisor have become what they were, no false embarrassment or fear prevented me to entrust him that I had taken advantage of so much confusion at the depot to load two truck instead of just one! No comment. Neubauer listened to my stories without a word, not approving nor disapproving of my procedures. Official process succeeding in getting unofficial supplies.

Back to the Kolkhoz with four bags of salt, changed for four barrels of butter and thirty bottles of vodka! Done.But the head of the Kolkhoz still wanted to drag me into his office for a'tete a tete'. In our area everything has changed. The command of the partisans was taken over by political commissars, experienced and ruthless. They are going to clean up the resistance. For now they check the advance of the German and Hungarian troops and make their report to the Soviet troops. Soon they will take action. I do not know how but tell your leaders to strengthen surveillance, especially at night.

The bottles of vodka and the butter barrels had their effect, but the confidential news from the head of the Kolkhoz dampened the spirits of my boss and the Works Leader: "Not a word of it to others. I will do the necessary." Neubauer was beginning to feel his good vodka and ordered dinner for the three of us, served in the Works Leader's office. I could not refuse!

I still had two hours to finish my article "Our Work Service men on all fronts."

The opening day of the mess hall has finally arrived. I recruited two bartenders and three servers that I knew. White jacket, white shirt and black bow tie - the tailor had done wonders. This put a touch of class in our inauguration.

At 6pm, everyone was on deck. Hors d'oeuvres at will and iced vodka. The Works Leader, Neubauer was in his uniform, as well as six company commanders. There were Aviation officers, including the chaplain. Anton and I had personally invited them. Apparently these fellows already are quite a bit high and the atmosphere could not be warmer. As 'MC' of the inauguration, I ask for a short silence for our Works Leader to make his welcome speech. In response, the Captain thanked his counterparts for the valuable military intelligence. I will not forget this part of speech ...

Let the festivities begin! Very elegant, my servers have the small sandwiches buttered bread with ham or herring, all accompanied by a glass of vodka. Amazement at the officer's table. Bread with real butter? Vodka? But how did you do it? With a knowing look, Neubauer replied simply: "No mystery when one has good organizers!"

Then the Colonel rises and everybody follows. Holding up his glass of vodka, a resounding toast: "To our friendship and long live our homeland, Prosit!" That's not a watered-down booze! All airmen choke! We knew better. Laughter broke out, and the long evening begins.

"Hey, this is jolly well organized here" whispered Anton.

"Anton, it's easy when we had the best example. I still have a favor to ask, I would like you to introduce me to the Commander."

"No problem, right now if you want."

"No, now it's party time!"

Four hours later, the airmen returned to their base singing. For some, it was the last chance to have a good time. The inauguration was a complete success.

The next day back to work! I'm off to the airstrip with my driver. With Anton I immediately address the issue of shipping the butter. "No problem, but do not forget to provide a package for the Colonel. We have air shipments twice a week, without control." Another issue close to my heart: could I come Sunday to the office with a couple friends?

"No problem. Meet me at 9am."

The day after the first packages were dispatched I did not fail to contact Willy Unverzagt to tell him that I will send two parcels with two boxes of cigars Dutch 'Willem II' one for him, one for my father.

Many other shipments would take place later, even after the departure of the squadron who transferred to another airport near Voronezh. "Our" airport was then reinforced early September to accommodate the much heavier Dornier bombers. The contacts between us and the pilots were not the same. The dragging on of the war began to be seriously felt. There were signs that could not be ignored. I thought back to the toast by the Colonel. He had raised his glass to drink to our friendship and our homeland without a word about the Führer!

After the inauguration of the officers mess hall was behind us, I could relax a little and focus on my journalistic function. I had the idea of a report on the work that our men did together with the army engineers to finish a road about ten kilometers from the front. On the clear summer days we worked as long as there was some light. Armored transport then took over all night. Knowing this, I am in no hurry. By late afternoon I reached the site, spotted an ideal hill and got out of the car to take pictures. I was just about to set my camera when the Russian artillery opened fire hitting the road haphazardly, probably to test the reaction of German and Hungarian positions. I was not about to ask so many questions but I threw myself into the first hole on the side without stopping to shoot blindly with my camera held up above my hideout. A glance to the car - nothing absolutely nothing! Pulverized by a shell. My driver? His body torn to a pulp. The shelling was as brief as lightning. Casualties litter the road. Ambulances run in all directions, giving first aid and leaving immediately for the Messerschmitt field hospital. I climbed on the last truck filled with corpses and the dying. I closed many eyes, with a prayer, drawing a sign of the cross on their forehead. The looks were twisted by pain or strangely absent, as if surprised by what they had lived through, as if they were not involved in their deaths.

The bodies were lined up in our camp, witness to the reality of war. Fifteen deaths of our Works Leader's comrades and seven army engineers. When he saw me coming down from the last truck, Neubauer gave me a hug. "There will be no story written on this."

*

Other than this frightful episode, it could be said that the summer was going smoothly. Many receptions in the officers' mess with everything perfectly prepared. The Messerschmitts went in groups of three or six aircraft to fly over the Russian positions and most returned safely.

One day, Anton called me and asked to see me. He asked me if I knew a certain Austrian, a mechanic responsible for preparing the Messerschmitts.

"Do I know him? Let's say I made a short trip by truck with him."

"Has he told you something about his political views?"

"No. Why?"

"Well, he was responsible for preparing a flight for the Colonel for an over view of the Russian lines. The first officer made a final check and discovered sabotage. He immediately informed the colonel asking the military police to investigate. In the locker room of the Austrian he found a book of Karl Marx. He was arrested and subsequently confessed to all that he was a Communist and that he would do everything possible to have Hitler lose the war. The military police sent him directly to a war tribunal and he was hanged for high treason yesterday morning. Now the police are looking for possible accomplices."

"So what? How does it affect me? Listen, Anton, I am a Catholic, not a communist, and last Sunday I attended the Mass of your Chaplain with four friends from my area."

I was not worried. I simply crossed out my draft article on Karl Marx and "Das Kapital".

June 28, 1942: Start of the great German offensive on Voronezh, dubbed "Operation Brunswick." Objective: to push the Red Army beyond the Volga River, the important supply route for the Soviets, especially for gasoline. Our Messerschmitts were actively involved. The 6th Army of General von Paulus took control over Stalingrad.

While all that was happening we spent the months of July and August on road repairs and preparing our airport for future Dornier bombers.

In mid-September the Works Leader calls for a meeting of the entire battalion with serious news. We will go under the command of the Wehrmacht. It's the end of an era. Imagining perhaps that I was privy to much more information because I was writing articles, my comrades from Hünfeld and Fulda pressed me with questions about the future. I knew little more than they did.

The officers and NCOs take the new orders and with the records of all members of the RAD transferred us into the Wehrmacht. I learned much later that almost none of my friends would come back alive. During the great Russian winter offensive of 1942-43 towards Kharkov, the infantry division to which they belonged was completely routed.

How did I escape their fate? In September of 1942, heaven came again to my rescue. Now in the Wehrmacht, I am one of four men to return to Germany: the Works Leader, Neubauer, the head chef and I, as a journalist. The typewriter, once more, saved my life.

The train that took us to our homeland was overflowing with soldiers on leave, back home for three or four weeks. I settled somehow in the hallway, sitting on my kit. One topic of conversation among travelers: war, always war. Rumors, beliefs, suppositions, all that could arise in the minds of men subjected to the tyranny of weapons related in a flood of words over the clanking of the rails. I kept a low profile. I was quite aware of the presence of the Gestapo spies infiltrating every corner of society. When we passed through Lemberg (Ukraine) I heard about the massacres of Jews. I thought of Mr. Hirsch, my father's friend.

At the Glauchau terminal, off to the barracks for payment of the final balance of our Work Service time, issuance of a certificate of completion of service and a train ticket home. Was it really over or just an intermission?

I announced my arrival to my parents by phone. My parents were waiting on the dock. Willy Unverzagt was there too, and I was very happy. As my parents had read some of my stories in the Hünfelder and Fulda newspapers they congratulated me. Then the questions. I had to tell and tell again. Time seemed to stand still. "How's Josef?" He is in the barracks in Fulda, he expects your visit.

The next morning I went to Fulda. At the barracks, a guard leads me to the administration building. My brother was in charge. I find him in his uniform of Staff Sargent, the highest rank of NCOs. We fall into each other's arms. Then he steps back to see me better,

"My word, you are damn grown up! You came into my type of army business!" It was true, since my departure for RAD I had grown an inch! "I missed our appointment at Kursk! I am lucky I'm still alive! Look."

He pulls down his uniform shirt. A large scar running the length of his back. "It is my leather equipment that saved my spine, otherwise I would be in a wheelchair." His right foot had also undergone several operations. His foot had regained it's basic form but it was paralyzed and slightly shorter than the other. My brother was limping slightly and was wearing orthopedic shoes. "For me the war is over. What about you?"

It was close to noon, I would tell Josef about my last six months over a meal in the brasserie on the corner. He immediately called a car. Everything came together for a good time. We were happy to be together.

Before leaving, I dropped in at the Schlitzer business school, but in vain: the director was not there. Pity. Anyway, the main task during these weeks of leave would be to visit everybody.

Our neighbor, the former Nazi, had just lost his third son. He was drafted into civil service under the army elsewhere in Germany. In another family, three boys were dead to the "madness of Hitler." During a visit with my father, he showed me the register of deceased persons. The majority of them had died for their country! Commenting on these sad statistics, he seemed be resigned to the worst, "This is only the beginning. Not only will that Austrian corporal make our country a field of ruins but we will be condemned by the whole world." With such sadness and discouragement on his face I did not have the heart to continue this conversation.

On December 9, we celebrated my birthday! 18 years! Some days later, a certified letter receipt, gave me my 'marching orders'. On January 3, 1943, I had to report to Eschwege, near Kassel. This still left me three weeks of 'freedom'. After Christmas and New Year, the military would take possession of all my moments. I was at an age where recklessness is the strongest force in our lives.

*

Chapter 3

France, sweet France!

January 3, 1943 fell on a Sunday. Obeying my working order, I introduced myself to the garrison of the 90th Infantry Division. Immediate registration at the office of regiment 261, confirming my incorporation to the 2nd Company, simple procedures of a well-oiled military organization.

In the military equipment building we are given our uniform, gun, gas mask and all the soldier's gear. We will be in a brand new barracks, six to a rooms, each with its locker. We put on our uniforms and at 1pm a NCO comes to take us for lunch. Twelve at a table. As always, the lunch is served family style. An officer is present. He was seriously wounded in the front of the East and named instructor for young recruits. He is warning us that in the Wehrmacht the familiar form is prohibited when addressing a superior, even vis-à-vis a simple corporal. A senior grade can of course use the familiar form when addressing a soldier.

My comrades were at least 19 because most had a higher education. Even though I was younger, I was the only one with a paramilitary experience. The officer stopped me after lunch and took me to the mess to introduce me to the section chiefs. These men were glad to hear of my adventures on the Russian front! For an hour, a game of questions and answers. Obviously this was not the place to tell of my success in the butter traffic! I told them instead of the relationships I had established with the airmen, including the ace, the Colonel with the Iron Cross. I had taken care to keep copies of my articles. I noticed in the eyes of my superiors that I had inspired respect. Finally, the sergeant accompanied me back to our building. He wished to continue the conversation: "Already in Russia at 17, you must not have been able to do much studying." I did not contradict him, but told him that because my father was not in agreement with Hitler's policies, I had to quickly enter the workforce. His career had similarities with mine: at 14 he worked on his father's farm near Marburg. With these mutual confidences it was clear we were on the same side.

On January 5 our battalion gathered in the courtyard to the take the oath. Again, I thought of my father, pretending to swear allegiance to the 'Austrian corporal'. Then the music covered everything with martial tunes.

In these winter days, and often at night, our life was entirely consumed with military training. In late February, five days of leave gave us the time for a brief family reunion. Only one question was on everyone's lips: where would we be sent? No one could answer. Barely back in Eschwege, we were informed that we would leave the barracks within eight days. Still nothing on the destination! I tried to pull it out of our sergeant and he relented on condition that I keep it to myself, "We're off to France, to continue training for at least eight months."

I was hoping to tell my family, but no way could I write about it. I took advantage of a Sunday afternoon to join my brother, and on his direct line and between platitudes, I gave them the news of my imminent departure for France. He typed: "Have fun." A few days before our departure we learned of the disaster of Stalingrad and the offensive launched by the Soviets on all fronts.

*

On 12 March 1943 our train of soldiers sped towards France. No time to be melancholy - we were young, and it seemed that we had lost sight of the real reasons for our presence in this train. We lived an adventure, that's all! We were careless, just happy to travel to what appeared to us like a land of plenty. 'Living like God in France!' That saying was in vogue in our compartments. Everyone went about telling his anecdotes. I had my brother in Brest. A whirlwind of images occupied our minds and, at the first stop in Verdun station, we rushed into a cafe to sniff a red wine accompanied by salami. Good bargain, you could pay in Reichsmarks. With other comrades I bought a bottle of wine and a sausage, promises of good times to come.

We now know what would be our final destination: Clermont-Ferrand. A column of trucks was waiting to transport us to our barracks. We were staying on the second floor of an old building in a large room holding forty soldiers, including four corporals. The showers were outside our room, luckily in the same block. I thought the French soldiers were not really spoiled! After placing our gear under our beds, we had time to go around our new 'home'.

At the center of the courtyard stood a monument to the dead of the Great War. Three black soldiers came in the uniform of the French army of 1914, they wore red caps as a hat. Why are they in our barracks? One of our friends ran to get his camera while we approach these men. One meets us in broken German: He's from Cameroon, a former German colony, while another, from Togo knows only French. All three are very friendly and we take pictures together. Then some 'students' of our section exclaimed, loud enough to be heard: "Look at that! They are photographed with Negroes!" Without answering, I looked at them to remember their faces, and then I warned my companions: "These guys are dangerous Nazi fanatics." My three friends understood - they were Catholics and we naturally stuck together. In war, the instinct to choose friends is very important for survival.

At 5 in the evening, the four companies met in the courtyard to form a perfect square. We were all ears: "Comrades, tomorrow will be devoted entirely to getting organized in our barracks. Your group leaders will section you and will detail your homework. The day after tomorrow will begin military training in the field. Pay attention to a few recommendations. We want you to always behave in an exemplary fashion. For trips into town, you have to be a minimum of three soldiers armed with your rifle or pistol. On the sidewalk, you step aside to let the French pass. Although we are an occupying army our behavior must be beyond reproach. If traveling in a train or tram, you will offer your seat to women and the elderly. For evenings out or on Sunday, you will be accompanied by an NCO. I wish you a good evening."

The next day, we were shown our 'daily chores' cleaning our room, showers, toilets, corridors, etc. These mandatory chores were also used for punishment. Violating the evening curfew, even when delayed by weather led to a sentence to clean the hallways with a toothbrush and liquid soap, as long as his superior demanded. Depending on the degree of humor of the NCO in charge, this could last until 4am for the unlucky soldier. At 6am wake up to the bugle. Fifteen minutes later, in the exercise yard, back, showered, in uniform, and breakfast. At 7.30 general inspection. Woe to him who had forgotten one of his things! It took us a week to get used to this routine.

The excellent contact I had with our NCO enabled me to have a clearer vision of the German forces in the region: an infantry division, a motorized division, artillery and tanks, a company of Flak air defense and a squadron of FW-190 fighter planes. The officer staff was grouped in the residential area of Royat. Soon we would have the opportunity to experience it all since the turn would come for us to be part of guarding the headquarters.

*

I kept a clear memory of our first military outing at the foot of the Puy-de-Dôme. An officer and a sergeant on horseback led the way followed by the section chiefs at the head of each company and then the NCOs with their groups. Along the way we sang military songs that we liked, hoping they would not offend the French. The windows were open along our way, people put the heads outside, and sometimes showed a certain welcome.

An entire army could maneuver on the training ground adorned with the colors of a huge field of spring flowers. But we were not there to enjoy the lovely French countryside.

For a few weeks, the same program: training in the use of arms, attack, shoot, camouflage, crawl to advance. It was an opportunity for me to remember the method that I developed for myself during our military training at Glauchau. During an attack on the enemy defense, we should never stay in the same place but after each firing of our guns we were told to roll ten feet sideways, so that a sniper would lose his target. By moving in zigzags, we could gain a hundred yards or so, and then do the same again. This method caught the eye of our NCO. He saw the ingenuity of my moves, and liked it enough to teach it to the entire group. The company commander asked me where I had learned this survival technique. "I learned it myself, it's only logical."

I was an excellent shot and I knew that I was to face the same good shots who would only be waiting to put a bullet in my head.

To build our endurance, we were gradually leaving the plain fields for steep areas with the summit in sight. With all our gear on our back, we had to attack up one mile of upward slopes. Halfway, we were exhausted. However, from day to day, our strength grew.

At the barracks a large room, divided in two, had been set up for combat training in case of a poison gas attack. Use of a gas mask is really difficult. Breathing is very painful, we must resist the temptation to unscrew the filter to gasp for some air. At the end of a training day, we were exhausted.

Then the day of exercise in real conditions came. At 7am, our battalion leaves by truck for the Puy-de-Dôme, a huge massive mountain rising 300 feet above the hills. Each company takes a position halfway up the top with forty kilos of equipment on the back. Then NCOs begin to scream: "Alarm gas! Gas alarm!" Just before we break out our gas masks the explosions release a yellowish smoke. Immediately, we put on our gas masks and we rush to the 'attack' a supposed enemy to occupy the heights. After a mere two hundred yards of the uphill race we are out of breath. The soldiers gasp for air, but our leaders yell "forward and faster, faster!" We are moving between the abandoned vineyards, gaining height somehow, and when we reach our goal, five hundred yards higher, we collapse and tear off our masks. Phew! NCOs are taking roll call. Three missing soldiers. They are found in the vineyards, not moving, struck down by a heart attack. Two of them could be saved. The third will not return. After this, gas masks will be practiced less.

To tell the whole story I should not fail to mention the pleasures offered to the Clermont-Ferrand Wehrmacht soldiers: Three weekly sessions of cinema with the entire theatre reserved for us, with French films of the interwar period, mostly comedies with German subtitles. We laughed at the jokes by Fernandel and many others.

Not surprising, we had very lively discussions among ourselves about the many French brothels that specialized in luring German soldiers, mostly officers, into their lairs. I had taken a liking to Laurent, an Alsatian volunteer who served as interpreter for our regiment, especially in the dealings between the German and French military police. We hit it off and often went out together. He said: "Brothel owners work hand in hand with the Resistance to buy themselves redemption after the end of the German occupation. They provide free girls to senior officers of both sides with the objective to obtain information. Our young soldiers are befriended in the streets by German speaking resistance fighters, often Alsatian students. They are invited into their brothels and, more than once, never would emerge! Dying in a brothel! Strange way to serve the Fatherland!"

"Those that came out alive tell their comrades of the extraordinary moments they have experienced. Six soldiers have already disappeared. The Gestapo and the French police have doubled their joint efforts to unravel the mystery of the disappearances. Watch out!"

These war brothel stories never failed to reveal new episodes. Once the Resistance had attacked a brothel attended by Germans soldiers by throwing gasoline containers against it and ignited them. Firefighters and French police quickly intervened to extinguish the flames, treat the burns, and to question witnesses. The car of the resistance fighters was found near the cathedral. From then on the atmosphere was tense.

Sunday, with friends, we decided to attend mass at the cathedral. Laurent accompanies us. We are armed only with our P38 pistols. We take the tram to the Cathedral Square and we slowly head towards the church. Suddenly, I feel an intense burning in the neck. Blood flows. Laurent immediately gets his First Aid kit. A friend points the finger towards the bell tower of the Cathedral: "They shot from there!" Laurent calms everyone: "No! Aloÿs cut himself with this bush branch." We double quick and take the first tramway and returned to the barracks. What should we say? Laurent convinced us to keep quiet, otherwise there will be reprisals and, as always, innocent lives will be lost. I agreed with him. "Did you hear or see anything? Me? Nothing."

We went to the battalion hospital. The doctor immediately realized what incredible luck I had: "One thenth of an inch more and your artery would have ruptured. It was a good shot." "Not a shooter, just the branch of a bush of thorns!" The doctor pretends to swallow this tall tale. "Yes, yes, Of course. I'll make my report accordingly, but be very careful. There are already enough deaths in Clermont-Ferrand." Yes, there was a tense atmosphere. Guards around our barracks, the headquarters of the regiment and division was strengthened, as well as the patrols day and night in the streets of the city.

The quiet life in France was over for us. The occupation was hardening. On a Sunday in June 1943 when we were about to leave I notice two strange groups under heavy guard in a corner of the courtyard. Curious, we approach but a voice dissuades us to go further: "Look as if you were watching the memorial." "Who are you?" "We are students from the University of Strasbourg. When Hitler invaded France, most students and teachers took one of the last trains to Clermont where we thought we could continue our studies. Many of us have played the hero and have carried out attacks against the German army, and they killed two members of the Gestapo in Vichy. Result, there has been a first roundup of students, followed by a protest march of 1500 students in the city center. The German army has not lifted a finger, but the militia and police arrested many demonstrators. Here we are about two dozen, but in the prisons of the Militia there are many more. Maybe we'll be shot tomorrow."

*

A few days later a train took us to Mende to join a motorized battalion. Everyone knew that the Resistance was well organized in Lozère while the prefect, the gendarmerie and the police collaborated with the Wehrmacht to maintain security.

In Lozère, I discovered the existence of forced labor for French men and women to work in Germany. That intrigued me a lot. Most young French sought to avoid this service imposed by the German Ministry of Labour and supported by the Vichy government. The most amazing to me was that even the Bishop of Mende urged young Catholics to go into this forced labor service. The Lozère Labor Unions openly condemned it. This unholy collaboration of the Bishop with the French militia, the police and the Gestapo, not to mention the policy of denunciations encouraged by Vichy was distasteful to most German soldiers,

Catholic or not. Many thought that this type of misbehavior showed a desperate attempt to forestall the inevitable that Hitler may already have lost his war.

German soldiers swarmed everywhere. Many of them, back from maneuvers, were to rest for several weeks. It is our turn to join the maneuvers. The first exercise was to teach us how to ford a river, a natural obstacle that we had to cross before organizing a new line of defense. The crossing was to be barefoot, with boots and socks hanging around our neck.

That day, I was elected to carry the support frame of a heavy machine gun: thirty kilos, which had to be added to my gun, ammunition, and the gas mask. The riverbed was covered with uneven stones. I slipped on a big stone, but only with my desperate contortions could I manage not to completely lose balance. Once on shore, the pain in my ankles forces me to call the nurse and I showed her my feet. They are a swollen mess! The doctor's verdict: "The maneuvers are over for you." He ordered my dismissal to Clermont-Ferrand, in the care of his colleague in the military hospital. Farewell Lozere, and without regrets!

In Clermont-Ferrand, a promotion was waiting for me: I was now a corporal, transferred to the regiment supply service staff.

Soon after, another surprise. We were to be given a few days of recovery furlough - to Paris!

*

Paris! The City of Light welcomed me with howling sirens and air defense gunfire guided by huge floodlights. False alarm: the bombers were only flying over the French capital towards Germany. For the first time, I could see the silhouettes of these huge flying fortresses in the sky. As the letters of my family had told me, the Allies bombed Germany and increasingly targeted arms factories. I was absorbed in the present moment, in these six days of 'vacation' in Paris.

Paris was for us all a mythical city. We follow the classical route: the Eiffel Tower, the Arc de Triomphe, the tomb of the Unknown Soldier, Montmartre and the Moulin Rouge (without being allowed to enter), cheap small restaurants, and then climbing up to the Sacred Heart where we were able to attend Mass in one of the chapels. The service was in Latin, and we could pray and sing in unison with the faithful.

The French capital seemed to exist solely for the pleasure of discovery: the Opera, Notre Dame, the Isle Saint-Louis. Our military Paris base was on Marbeuf Street, two hundred yards from the Champs Elysées, a hotel just for us soldiers. There were receptions held by a hotel officer assisted by German secretaries. The large restaurant could seat at least four hundred, with service from 5am to midnight. This military hotel, very well organized, could accommodate four to five hundred soldiers from the provinces before they would return the next day for their barracks elsewhere in France. A large reading room and a German film theatre completed this bee hive of constant comings and goings. This hub was a great way for us to spend our precious time in Paris.

Then the obligatory window shopping on the Champs-Elysées, the buying of small souvenirs, people watching while sipping a coffee on the sidewalk, the days flying away without a moment of boredom. 9pm! Already! We rushed into the subway to Vincennes. At 10pm, everyone had to be in the barracks.

Last day at our home away from home. Between German soldiers and Parisians, the subway was packed. I walked a lot, immediately noticed by the hotel officer who invited me to a champagne lunch. "You will not regret it, it's excellent! It was a specialty of my restaurant back home." He ordered a bottle, slices of bread and ham, together with scrambled eggs and then a toast to our health "and especially that we find our families again healthy and sound!"

What a great lunch! For the first time I tasted a very good French champagne. My newly found friend had been in the First World

War until 1917 when he was injured, returned to Germany and took over the hotel and restaurant of his father, near Mainz. At the end of 1940, the army had recruited him to organize this military home on the Rue Marbeuf: "Now I am 52 years old, widowed for two years and you, you are only 18! I lost two of my three sons. The third is married, has two children and with his wife he runs our hotel and restaurant. Do you know why I'm telling you all this? Because your papers state that you are a Catholic. I, too, am a Catholic. We will never be on their side. Yes, but you have to be very careful: Traitors are everywhere and the Gestapo pays well." A long silence followed, before the officer resumes: "I have made all my arrangements. The night life of the most senior members of the Nazi Party in Paris has no secrets for me. The Wehrmacht generals and senior officers of the SS are invited by bankers, often Jewish, to great evenings in mansions or for hunting in Sologne. I have my sources. The cream of the army and the SS are lodged in the best places."

The meal was finished. Shake hands. "Maybe we'll see each other back home one day!"

Last walk on the Champs-Elysées. I met soldiers visibly delighted to spend a week of vacation in Paris. There were all these swastikas flags. The biggest of them was displayed under the Arc de Triomphe. Everywhere propaganda banners, including the Opera House façade. In large letters it read: "Germany will win!" I thought this kind of display was unnecessary and a very cruel provocation. Before becoming swallowed up by the subway, I had time to see a parade of the latest German tanks: the famous Tiger Panzer. It was a sunny evening. At 7pm I was back in the barracks. The following day at 4pm back in Clermont - Ferrand.

*

The head physician at the hospital confirms that I had to wear hard orthopedic shoes for one more week, night and day. Once recovered, I joined the Royat supply staff with my new rank of corporal. The officer who welcomed me invited me to join him for a drink.

In the cafe there were a dozen soldiers and a few civilians. The atmosphere was friendly. I found Laurent who taught us to toast in French and we applied the lesson by repeating in chorus: "Sante'!" One of the Frenchmen then said to Laurent in German, with a strong Eastern French accent: "Hey you, Laurent, now you teach them French?"

On the way back Laurent warned us: "Be careful when you are in a bar or cafe. The walls have ears. Never talk about your military activity, just emphasize the good life in France, the kindness of the French. The guy who spoke in German with his Alsatian accent is an old professor of the University of Strasbourg. He is not happy to live here, he prefers his college."

The next evening, Laurent invites me to take a glass of white wine: "After dinner, we go to a little cafe, very friendly, where we can talk quietly." He was right. The bistro was not very big. There was no German military. I recognized the university professor and immediately, to my surprise, two Alsatian students from our barracks. By what miracle were they here? No miracle, but the result of a coup, planned carefully. When transferred to a prison of the Militia or the Gestapo, a commando of the Resistance had attacked their trucks, distributed weapons and released all prisoners except three killed by the militia. Not a single policeman or French police officer had lifted a finger.

I congratulate the Alsatian students. What has a German soldier like me to do in the midst of these men? Laurent had to feel bad for putting me in a very uncomfortable position. He wanted to lighten the mood by a loud: "Sante!" and "let's talk about something else. According to one student, the grape harvest 1943 would surely be as good as 1942: You will soon have the best grapes for dessert at the barracks." He said that with some kind of sly look.

Laurent leaves with one of the Frenchmen. Seeing them talk out there, I get the feeling that this man is not a pillar of virtue.

Back inside the cafe Laurent whispers in my ear that these guys are his superiors, his chiefs of the resistance. Knowing my anti-Nazi beliefs, he had asked them to accept me into their group. Laurent will not return to the barracks, he decided to desert to the Resistance. In order not to arouse suspicion, he left all of his belongings in the barracks. "Are you ready to join us?" The question came clear and sharp. No hesitation on my part either, "Listen Laurent, you are French, you will be with the French to fight the German occupiers. I am a German soldier and while I detest the Nazis that does not mean that I would betray my country. Even if I did, the Resistance would always look at me askance, a deserter who cannot be trusted. I cannot accept your proposal."

The problem now was that we had gone to the cafe together, and our names have been registered. I suggest you come back to the barracks with me, we will offer a bottle of wine to the barracks guards so that they will properly record our return, and you will find a way to go back to the cafe to join your comrades. "Your absence will not be noticed until tomorrow and by then you will be long gone. I will keep quiet."

The next evening, the section chief wondered about Laurent. We had not seen him all day. Do I know anything? I told them that we had a drink together the day before and then I returned, that's all. The section chief invited me to dinner at the mess. For dessert, we had white grapes. The platoon leader saw my surprise: "Nice grapes, right?" I was thinking back at the hours spent in the small bistro, trying to find certain details, such as a remark by the Alsatians about grapes. I remembered the strange smile of the one who had told me about the next grape delivery.

The next day September 27, 1943, our company received the order to secure a road block about ten miles away, with a dozen soldiers. At the dinner table, the sergeant tells me to leave with half of the patrol in half an hour. He would join us a little later with the rest in a second vehicle. The meal happily consumed we enjoyed the beautiful white grapes - a delight. At our control point half an hour passes. The second car is still not there. At 8pm, we can't wait any longer and called our company. Strange, the offices are nearly empty. The receptionist told us that all the officers were invited to a grand reception in town. All this seems very strange. A soldier then comes running, screaming: a guard writhing in pain on the ground. Soon, all hell breaks lose. A second man is overcome by some horrible malaise, then a third, yet another. Then my turn - I feel a surge of lightning fever, headache, nausea. I called for help to division headquarters: "Quick! Tell all positions, I think we have been poisoned! Forbid everyone to eat grapes! Quick!" My head is spinning, confused, images jostle, Laurent, small bistro, Alsatians, "Sante!" White grape deliveries. Then nothing.

Upon awakening, I was served breakfast, soup and two rolls. I was in a hospital. Since when? A man in a white coat approached my bed: "The 1st infantry company has been poisoned, the alarm was raised eighteen days ago. I work at the artillery hospital, next door in a former camp for German prisoners. When the first patients arrived, I thought they would not come out alive. The analysis of physicians is clear: poisoning, probably typhoid virus injected into the white grapes. As the alarm arrived quickly, the grapes were immediately removed."

"Clermont-Ferrand has become an entrenched camp. Controls everywhere, armored and artillery occupied all key posts in the German army. We even saw Tiger tanks rolling to Clermont-Ferrand. During the first two weeks, you and your comrades were all in a daze. Bodies burning with fever, clothes soiled with urine and loose stool. Some, like you, fought with superhuman strength. The doctor came twice a day for a bit, you were flailing like a drowning man. We had to tie you to the bed."

It was true. Snippets of images came back to me. In my delirium I could see this doctor, horrible, deformed, with huge glasses and a monstrous syringe. It terrified me, and I believe I screamed in fear. That's right, the nurse confirmed that one night you got to free yourself, you got out of bed, you put your helmet on shouting: "Save yourselves, we are under attack!" We caught you and put to bed with a double dose of sedative. Then another day, the doctor noticed your rosary around your neck with a medal of the Virgin. Before you could do it yourself, he asked a nurse to place it in your hands. You kissed the cross murmuring: Lady protect me!"

I was recovering slowly. The daily schedule never varied: morning shower, supported by a nurse while they changed the sheets and mattress. Back in bed, clean nightgown, injections, sleep. The occupants of other beds succumbed, one by one. Only wrestlers survived. I asked a nurse: "How many are dead?" She would not reply. Three weeks passed in this fashion. Finally, after a final check by the health service I was released.

My company section chief completed the story. When I had given the alert, the my sergeant with seven men were on their way to Royat. The driver took violently ill, lost control of the vehicle and hit a tree. Just then a Renault had shown up from nowhere with resistance fighters who killed all our soldiers. When they fled they got caught in a road block of the French and German police who immediately opened fire. Two of the four resistance had tried to flee but a third was killed and the fourth turned his gun against himself ... No one would be taken alive. No IDs, no witnesses, the dark of the night covered everything.

My section chief filled me in. Although the grapes had been removed immediately after the alert I had sounded, one hundred fifty-two men had been poisoned, twentyfour had died. The section chief shook my hand warmly, "Tomorrow you get back to the barracks and you will be received by the head of the battalion."

The next day, the battalion commander, in the presence of all the officers, congratulated me for my courage and presence of mind. My response had saved the lives of many of our comrades. The colonel delivered the epilogue of this dirty business. The original delivery of grapes had been intercepted by the Resistance who killed two of our men by shots in the head. Then these guys inoculated the virus into the grapes - a cowardly act.

Turning to me: "Tomorrow you check into a spa near Saint-Etienne, Chatelguyon, for three weeks. Then you are entitled to four weeks of leave with your parents. Best wishes for your future."

Quick calculation, three weeks, four more: I will perhaps celebrate Christmas with my parents!

*

Chapter 4

A Bittersweet Christmas at Home

After my convalescence in Châtel Guyon, I was sent back to the barracks of Eschwege. Nice surprise: I was made sergeant. My officer informed me that soon I will get my future destination by registered letter: "In the meantime, celebrate your birthday with your parents and perhaps Christmas."

A small detour to the administration, some formalities, and I am on the first train leaving for my home town Hünfeld.

Before crossing back from France into Germany, there was a six-hour layover in Mulhouse, a chance to spend my last Reichsmarks for gifts for my family. I had never met my sister-in-law Hedwig, Josef's new wife. What to get for her? I decided on a turquoise gown, the only one left in the shop. When I showed it to Josef after arriving in Fulda, he cried out: "This is madness! It is perfect for Hedwig, especially since she has blue eyes." Being a little indiscreet, I asked him about his married life. As he could not be away from the barracks, Hedwig joined him in Fulda, from Saturday to Wednesday. She was staying at a hotel, just opposite the barracks. Since there was always the possibility of bombing of the big Fulda tire plants she was afraid to stay there.

Arriving at the station in Hünfeld, nobody was there to meet me and no taxi. So I walked the mile to my parents' home with my bag of gifts where I was greeted my sisters Clara and Catherina. It was on December 1, Clara's birthday. By wishing her the best, I added that we would be celebrating mine in a few days with my parents. Later, I held them in my arms and got to know Hedwig, my new sister-in-law. I enjoyed playing Santa with my gifts, to their protestations "This is too much! Here we hardly ever find anything any more." Hedwig was most embarrassed by my gift: "It really was not necessary but the gown is wonderful!" My mother decided to immediately serve the real coffee I had unearthed in Mulhouse. Real coffee!

Meanwhile our friend Willy Unverzagt had appeared. Anni, my sister, was not there, unable to get away from her hotel school, twenty miles from Hünfeld, a school run by six Oblate nuns. The convent of the Oblate fathers had been dismantled by the Nazis and turned into a military hospital, the monks arrested by the Gestapo and deported to a camp as anti-Nazis! As for the nuns, they were kept in place and became nurses. The questions came from all sides on how it was for me being a soldier and now an NCO. What was there to tell? I emphasized the positives. For my parents, the key was that I was there to spend Christmas with family.

After coffee with Willy Unverzagt, my father and our neighbor retired into the living room to have a man to man talk about the country's situation. The Nazi terror was spreading into the countryside. The police and the Gestapo were attacking farmers accusing them of supplying the black market, and not respecting the law which obliged them to deliver their entire production to the agricultural cooperative. Many were arrested for their supposed resistance, and often beaten.

My mother's sister had a large farm in one of the nearby villages. Since the death of her husband in 1938, she had entrusted the operation to their third son, Amand, who was a year older than I. He was exempted from military service after the death of his two brothers on the Russian front. The eldest, Aloysius, had died in December 1941 before Moscow. Edmond, my other cousin, was a bright young man, very musical. He was drafted in 1942 in the gendarmerie which, according to the sub-prefect and the mayor, seemed reassuring: it would not be first in line. In fact, the first letter from Edmond was not too frightening for my aunt. In a second letter, he wrote that the camaraderie within the Einsatzkommando was excellent and that their training would be completed shortly. In his third letter, rather briefly, he revealed the true activity of the commando: burning villages, hunting and killing Jews, often with the cooperation of Polish collaborators. Edmond was unconsolable. He ended with these words: "May God forgive me, but I'd rather die." A few days later an official letter informed my aunt that Police Officer Edmond Wassermann had "succumbed to his injuries." For me it was clear: either he had killed himself or he had refused to carry out orders and was executed by firing squad. I did not say what was in the back of my mind, but I advised Amand to keep those letters that one day could be useful.

I tried to see everyone during my furlough. How much sadness, everywhere, in this month of December 1943! So many mothers mourning their sons, women their husbands.

Our neighbor had a terrible time. His fourth son had died three months earlier, exempted from military service but forced to work in a munitions factory in Kassel. Goebbels, the Nazi Minister of Propaganda, had organized a large rally and called for total war to ensure the final victory of the German Reich. This 'total war' fell very much on Kassel leaving tens of thousands of civilians dead!

I never failed to visit the families of my Work Service comrades who had shared my life in Russia in 1942, before all were being sent to the Eastern front. Each time, they showed me the same letters: "Died for the Fatherland and for our Führer Adolf Hitler." All the families had kept the newspapers with my articles and the photos of their sons and preserved them as relics. People were happy to see me because their sons had often told them about me. They were anxious, they expected me to tell them when the war would end. How would I know? All I could do was to give them some hope for a rapid solution!

The father of a friend who runs a construction company called Fladung and Son had been a member of the Nazi party in 1933. This earned him many advantages in the awards of public works contracts. The news of the death of his eldest son, in early January 1943, had overcome him. He had counted on him to take over his business one day. Then, in September of that year, when his second son came home, disfigured, one leg and one arm torn off, he became furious. At the regional office of the Nazi Party he had torn his party membership card to pieces and threw his party badge on the desk screaming, "You are murderers! You took the life of two of my sons!" He could not stop screaming until the Gestapo came to imprison him. At that moment, he had only one thought: "Let them kill me too." Finally released, he came back and wanted to take care of the second son, completely incapacitated. As for his business, at the end of 1944 the Allies would bomb the Fulda and the Hünfeld train stations where the Fladung company was located, to be wiped off the map.

I remembered the tailor, the one I had managed to sell a magazine subscription for the 'Stadt Gottes' as he strutted in front of the church on Sundays in his black SS uniform. He entered the Waffen-SS in 1942, was shipped to the Eastern Front in October. His wife told me every week he was sending a letter, but then for four weeks nothing. To reassure her it was easy to tell her the truth: when a division is sent to a new area, every one was forbidden to write. Maybe his letters will come later. There is one thing to wish: perhaps he found faith and may God protect him.

- How are your girls? What are they doing?

"The oldest was working at the Fulda hospital as a nurse. At 18, she was drafted in the army and is in a military hospital in eastern Poland. In her last letter she said that everyone is drowning in blood. Twice they had to flee in panic in the trucks of the Red Cross with their wounded. The nurses are scared of falling into Russian hands where a horrible fate would await them."

*

On December 9 I celebrated my 19th birthday. My mother had prepared the traditional German 'coffee and pastry' afternoon and a birthday cake but somehow the joy of the celebration was not there. My father was depressed: "Already four years that the Austrian corporal is leading Germany into the abyss. We all will be banished by the world and universally dishonored." No one knew how to break the silence that fell after these words. Willy Unverzagt tried with a little story: "The other day at the cinema I saw a documentary of the great rally of Goebbels in Kassel, in the Henschel arms factory. The aim was to mobilize the German people to fight with all their strength and to support Adolf Hitler until the final victory. There were not enough available Nazis for the rally! So they ordered the plant management to round up all the factory workers, women, men and to line them up in the huge hall and told them to shout: Heil! Heil! Heil! With arms raised. All this to illustrate the slogan of the Nazis: "One people, one country, one Fuehrer!" and to show the world national unity in the news images. Then every one in the world will say: the Germans are all Nazis!" Then the fourth son of our neighbor, Wigbert, was killed in this very factory during the next bombing by the Allies, just a few days after this speech by Goebbels. More than 20,000 dead! Was this mentioned on the radio or in the cinema? This Hitler war is lost ... but it is not over."

I asked my father if he had any news of his business friend Mr. Hirsch. In spring, Hirsch's plant supervisor had appeared with a van full with leather and fabrics. He said that his boss had told him if anything would happen to him to deliver these goods to my father, no cost. He also conveyed the thanks of his boss for my father's friendship and the help that he had given to him and many other Jews. He was sending his blessing. My mother asked the supervisor if he wanted to stay for dinner. No, he set off again immediately to try to see his boss. For three days Hirsch was held in his own home in house arrest by the Gestapo. They had confiscated his colonel's uniform, his decoration, his pistol. "For your next trip, you won't need it," the Nazis had said. Before hitting the road, the supervisor had promised my father to call to keep him informed. Okay, but be careful on the phone! Two days later, my father received a phone call, very brief "Hello, from a friend. Unfortunately, I did not find your friend. He went on a journey."

The mood was leaden as if a satanic stench had permeated the atmosphere. Yes, the Satan and the Devil do exist, and in our days his name was Adolf Hitler or Josef Stalin, the porters of death.

I often saw Willy Unverzagt and we talked freely. But why does he still wear his party badge? He told me he was ashamed to do so but he remained a member of the Nazi Party at the request of my father. I thought that given the ever present threat by the Nazis he had done the wise thing, as distasteful it might be for him.

We knew the war was lost, but it was not over. God only knew what was in store for us in 1944. The Americans did not seem in a hurry to move into Germany. They had landed in Africa and their next step would be Italy, or perhaps the south of France. As to the generals of the High Command of the Wehrmacht, they lived in the old tradition of the German Empire: "God with us", and loyalty to the Leader and the Fatherland. No one dared break his oath, even considering that it was to this unsavory guy Hitler they had sworn fidelity.

I opened myself up to Willy Unverzagt: "For two years I have participated in this madness. I can tell you that the majority of soldiers are not at all convinced of the abilities of the great 'war strategist Hitler.' I hope the day will come when the generals and brave officers will take action to stop this nonsense. I know the terror the Nazis are using to enforce their insane laws and that this is why you, my father and many others must at all costs hold on to your Christian morality in the hope that the day will come when you will be needed to help in the rebuilding of our country. I promised my father and my mother that I will do everything I can to return home and I pray to God and the Virgin Mary to protect me. Christmas is coming soon. In the meantime let's celebrate the holiday as we have always done."

I said the same thing to my father. I wanted to persuade him not to give up in despair and to celebrate the Nativity as we have always done:

"Yes, let's celebrate Christmas. Sure! For years at midnight mass, Unverzagt was at the organ, the children sang Christmas carols, there were men and women choirs. Today Midnight Mass is prohibited. It will take place the day after the Nativity, followed by the shepherds' procession, but only inside the church. You saw the streets are no longer lit."

- Well Father, we will celebrate Christmas as we always did, at Christmas Eve and Christmas Day at church. Then we will have our Christmas meal.

- Aloysius, don't you see that times have changed? We simply cannot do as we wish.

- OK, Father, but we will in any case spend Christmas together as a family as before. And so we did, an island of peace and happiness in the midst of infernal repression.

A week before Christmas I received a registered letter. I had to report on January 3rd at a special training camp at Wildflecken, a small town not too far from home.

Snow had fallen and it was very cold, like a picture-book Christmas. I visited my aunt and my farmer cousin Amand to present my best wishes and I asked them if they would sell me two geese. My cousin did not want to hear about money: "It will be our gift." I thanked him a thousand times.

One goose was for us and one for Willy Unverzagt. My little sister Anni had gotten permission to be with us until the New Year. My brother Josef and his wife Hedwig were also with us. Knowing that I would spend the next few months in nearby Wildflecken gave us some consolation.

To prepare me for the cold of Wildflecken, my mother found woolen underwear for me. I protested a bit to be mothered like that but when we got there the evening of January 3, 1944, I was glad because the wind was icy. Buses were waiting to take us to our barracks and I took my place where it said 'NCOs'. It was a temporary accommodation for the night.

The next day, assembly in the great hall, with a little over two hundred NCOs and officers. A major, surrounded by four officers welcomes us to Wildflecken, one of the largest military training camps in Germany rumored to be one of the toughest. Looking fit and energetic and covered with decorations, Major von Kleist addressed us. He had lost an arm in 1942 with one of the first German troups sent to Finland. Together with the Finns his division defended the long border with Russia. During the 42-43 winter, they had harassed and attacked the Red Army in small units, especially at night. In late April 1943, severely wounded, he had spent three months in a military hospital in Helsinki, before his return to Germany.

The Major explained our training program: "You will receive your winter equipment today. Your weapons will be treated with a special oil that works well even at -40 F. Skis and boots are for Nordic skiing. For three weeks all NCOs will be trained by experienced officers. This workout is not primarily an exercise for the winter war, but for endurance. You NCOs, you are the core of the army. By training young recruits, you must be like a father to them who inspires confidence. Your conduct should be exemplary, your decisions clear and precise. When attacking the enemy you will always be the first to attack and the last to retreat."

He pauses for a moment as to give more weight to his words: "The army that wins is an army that has total confidence in its superiors, from the sergeant to the highest command." Somehow his speech left me with the strange feeling that he did not have much confidence in the high command!

Three weeks of hellish training followed. We were divided into groups of thirty-five NCOs, under the command of an officer and submitted to unrelenting exercises, at least two were held overnight. A small spade had reappeared in our equipment for digging shelters in the compacted snow. Back in the barracks, on Saturday night, we were totally exhausted. The following Sunday was the only day off from these maneuvers. In the evening, a team was going to ski back for resupplies. Three weeks into these tough exercises we had lost many pounds but gained in muscles and especially in endurance. We were ready to become instructors.

Young recruits arrive, some 18 years old, most 17. I have ten men under my command. They have their winter gear and have received the rudiments of military training. I was aware that I was now on the other side of the fence, so to speak. First, sharing an evening meal with them. While there was a lieutenant and a sergeant at the table, it is for me to set the tone.

I quickly saw that there were two types of soldiers: those who want to fight with conviction, not to miss the 'final victory', and the others who are just following orders. In these conditions it is a delicate job to create a team spirit. Avoiding politicization I had to find the right words: "My life as a soldier told me that an army, a division or a company needs a leader, a leader who inspires confidence in his subordinates by his example. To be leader you must first learn to obey, especially in times of war. In the coming weeks, I will show you how to defend your life, how to overcome the enemy, but also how to rescue a wounded comrade and not to leave any one behind."

Let's go! For two months I work to train my men, lead them in war games, giving them a maximum of endurance. They suffer but I give them my example. In mid-February, they are trained in shooting lying down or while moving. Last Friday of the training they remove their skis for a static exercise as sharpshooters. The shooter who reaches 80% of the total points, from different distances, is entitled to a weekend leave. Although I shoot over 80% points, I'll stay with the group and we will spend the afternoon and the next day in a school setting for theoretical instructions.

In late February Major von Kleist called all the officers and NCOs to our mess hall to announce our imminent departure. He wanted to congratulate us for the excellent training we gave the young recruits and that we definitely deserved the title of 'cradle of the army'. Then: "I will not go with you, I will have to stay at Wildflecken. I wish you a safe return to Germany."

The die is cast... In early March our battalion leaves for the Marburg barracks. We are four hundred men, four companies. A few days after our arrival we gather in the courtyard in rows of five. An NCO does the roll call and then gives orders to two rows to advance ten steps. I am not a part of this group: the sergeant stopped to count just before my row. Too bad, this selection separates me from one of my friends from Wildflecken. I'd like to join his group. Several soldiers have also changed groups without triggering a protest. Discretly, I advance to the first group. Then some Chief Warrant Officer I had not noticed before ordered me back to take my original place. I protested that other soldiers had exchanged theirs. No discussions, that's an order! Disgruntled, I take my original place. An officer comes to us. Each soldier is in suspense to hear his destination from the lips of this ranking officer, as if waiting for a verdict to fall: "Group I goes to the eastern front." The group in which I stayed in spite of myself is sent to Italy.

In our group, joy broke out while a dead silence falls over the other group. We learn later that these soldiers were routed in Sevastopol or captured. Very few survived to see their home again.

I was stunned by the confluence of circumstances. No doubt: I had received last minute divine protection. I thanked God with all my heart. I also wanted to find that Chief Warrant Officer who had saved me from my own rash move. He was nowhere to be found - I was convinced that my guardian angel had not forgotten me and that the way the sorting of the soldiers had happened was a sign from heaven, as if a voice had said to me: "Go thy way, it is done, and nothing will change for you there."

*

Chapter 5

Enchanting Italy - but Not for Me!

"It's not always easy to reach port!"

Our trip to our new destination in Italy was not straight foreward. For starters, we were immobilized for a week trying to cross into Italy in Austria's lively Tyrol Mountains. The Allied had bombed the Brenner railway line. We finally arrived in Verona in mid-April, harassed by Allied aircraft all the way. In Bologna we said farewell to the train: the Allied bombs had finally rendered the rail line Bologna-Florence-Rome totally impassable.

Already in early 1944 the Americans had absolute control of the sky. Everywhere, relentlessly, there were US planes. Just once I saw a German plane, a "Fieseler Storch", a slow moving German single-engine reconnaissance aircraft. In this specific case, it was to carry a general to a hospital ...

We continued our way south on trucks and to Orvieto in the Tuscany wine country.

It was late April 1944, a Sunday. We were put into an old school building. Free time until 4pm. I decide to attend mass at the cathedral. First surprise: I had never seen such a striking church construction, all in long lines of alternating black and white stone. Mass had not yet started, the church was almost empty. I head to the altar of the Virgin Mary and pray a long time. Intensely. When

I turn around, the church is full! A man asks me to settle down in the front row obviously reserved for notables. At his side, two teenage girls and a very lovely woman. The man sought eye contact with her as he invited me to sit down. She silently indicated her consent.

Mass was unforgettable. I participated with my whole soul. The mass was said in Latin, abolishing the borders between nations. In my mind I was transported back to my home town, reliving our habitual Sunday mass, surrounded by my family, singing to the glory of God. At the great organ, Willy Unverzagt finished by raising our souls to heaven. In this Italian church, I was moved in the same way, forgetting my Wehrmacht uniform, forgetting that I was in a now hostile country. Wiping my tears, I realized that my neighbors were watching me with love and brotherhood. I was shocked and relieved when the mass ends.

I wanted to thank this man but it was he who spoke to me first and invited me to lunch! His wife nodded. He spoke German with a strong Italian accent. I accept their invitation happily, but worrying whether I would create trouble for them. The man reassured me. His first name was Gianluca, translated to me as Johannes Lukas. His eldest daughter is called Bianca Maria, a name as lovely as she is. This is my first contact with Italians and it could not be more engaging.

A large carved portal leads into their home. We crossed a courtyard with a fountain. It was a beautifully kept house, decorated with much taste, much care. Of course, I could at first only see the reception hall but it was enough to give me an idea of their whole beautiful home.

In the living room, they began by serving an aperitivo. For me I could not imagine a better setting. In the dining room, a superb table was set for six. We were only five! A young man then entered, with his father's stature combined with the beauty of the mother, certainly their son. Seeing me, he gives me a look full of hatred and leaves the room, immediately followed by his father. We hear the echo of a stormy discussion. Then the two men returned. This young man is the third son of my hosts, named Ricardo. I was seated at the head of the table, framed by the parents and by the sisters.

Clearly, the sight of my uniform is an insult to the son with an insurmountable disgust shown on his face. I asked permission to take off my jacket. My shirt is not ironed, but clean. The father translates my request, and permission, of course, is given. "Satisfied?" I asked Ricardo. He said nothing but his attitude softened somewhat.

I had never tasted more delicious dishes or drank a more remarkable wine. The father directed and translated the conversation. He is a lawyer but also a winemaker. Some of the best white wines of Orvieto come out of his basement and he does not hide his pride in being a supplier of wine to the Vatican. He acquired his knowledge of German at the University of Basel before his studies in Verona. As a young lawyer in Verona he met his future wife and a few months later sealed his love in the cathedral of Orvieto. His wife inherited a great winery from her father, and so her husband became a winemaker also.

After lunch, we go to the salon for an espresso and grappa. I was invited to talk about my childhood. My host never makes reference to Nazi Germany or the war, but our conversation seems timeless, simply human. I feel I am in a haven of peace. Speaking of my youth, however, I cannot help saying that, in fact, there was very little of it: Now at age 19, I had been under arms for two years. Gianluca interrupts me: "Did you volunteer?" "Volunteer? Certainly not! I was drafted!"

Inevitably, the conversation returns to the war. Until now, with God's help, I was able to escape the big massacre. Now, in Italy against a high-powered US military, I tell my host that I am under no illusions about the ability of the German army to withstand their assault. I go even further. If we fight, I will fight also, but I will not take any chances. I do not want to die for these bastard Nazis. I want to see my parents again, my family, my country. My fondest hope is that the Americans will end it quickly!

My remarks make my hosts very pensive. The father takes the floor, looking serious. Originally, their family consisted of four sons and two daughters. The two elder son died in 1942 at ages 27 and 22 years in North Africa. The youngest, like me 19 years, is fighting alongside the Americans. They have not heard from him for three months. As for Ricardo, he stayed in Orvieto to help Italy to get rid of his fascist compatriots and the Germans. Upon that, the whole family rallied. I am their enemy.

I do not understand. They invite me into their home. I had a delightful time, and then I learn that we are enemies. Gianluca interrupts me. They too had a good time with me. He and his family had watched me during mass. The intensity of my prayers had not escaped them. All my behavior during the service absolved me in their eyes. They said to themselves, "He is a man like us, he will never do wrong to someone." That is why they invited me. When they told me about their commitment to the Italian resistance, and especially that Ricardo is an active member, they knew I will not betray them. They wanted to make me aware that, in Italy, men are willing to sacrifice to regain the confidence of the free world, that confidence that they had lost in twenty years of Mussolini's folly.

Gianluca finished. It's time for you to leave, he said.

He knows as well as I the rules that require me to return to our barracks at 4pm. He even knows the rest of my program. That night, he tells me, I will go to Frosinone where my staff is located. Then I will be facing the front at Monte Cassino, or rather, Formica. I told them that we were under strict orders not to get anywhere near the Monte Cassino mountain, and under no circumstances were we allowed to enter the Monte Cassino monestary itself, having been declared an 'open city' as a cultural monument to be saved for the world.

He tells me that the great Allied offensive is about to be launched and, for the Germans, it will be a debacle. He offers me protection and refuge in his house if, in our retreat I would go through Orvieto.

76

For the moment, he commended me to God by squeezing both my hands warmly. His wife makes a sign of the cross on my forehead. The two girls and their brother shake my hand and wish that I will find my family again.

I was moved to tears, unable to find my words to express my gratitude and it was almost like fleeing as I leave the house. Only in their front yard I recovered enough to say a big 'thank you'. "I will never forget you!"

Gianluca was right. At sunset we go to Frosinone where we arrive on the 1st of May 1944. Our welcoming committees were Allied fighter-bombers. A surprise attack, and we already had many wounded in our ranks even though we were not directly targeted, but a nearby military warehouse was. We had to quickly join the main German positions on the other end of town.

At the registry office of the divisional General Staff they send me to Pontecorvo, next to Monte Cassino, when suddenly, a chief warrant officer burst into the office, "Your name is Pappert?" I am stunned: it is the NCO from Marburg, the very one who saved me from the eastern front! "You have a brother named Josef?" I mumble a yes. "Well, I did my military service with him. Come, I'll take care of you." Take care of me? Clearly it means protecting me. He tells the warrant officer to change my assignment. I'll be headed to the 94th division which will be replaced in mid-May and restructured in northern Italy. For now, I leave for Formia and Scauri. There, Major Hartmann, informed of my arrival, welcomes me. It remains for me to go through the usual office procedures to take my new command. Time to wish me luck and the NCO disappeared. I did all this without saying more than just three words.

Back at the registration desk, I ask if he knows the name of the sergeant. He does not know and who cares? The main thing is that I had escaped a very tight spot. My new group, heading for Pontecorvo, was to support the paratroopers of the first line of defense of Monte Cassino. In this sector, the fighting was intense. The loss in men and equipment is heavy but for the moment the

94th division is in a relatively quiet place. Besides it will be relayed mid-May.

Again, the miraculous intervention of this 'unknown' NCO had set me free. Again, this man had come out of the blue just when I was facing a great risk. More than ever, I thought of my guardian angel. I could see myself in a quiet corner, waiting for the guns finally falling silent.

We reach Formia without too much trouble. Major Hartmann receives me kindly and informs me of the next operations. I take command of a group of ten men and a scout. We go on foot to join the 2nd Battalion at Scauri.

We get going at nightfall. After five or six miles we take a dirt road that leads us to a large farmhouse converted into a food warehouse and a medical unit. We eat a good lentil soup, bacon, sausage and our dark army bread. A convoy of four mules accompany us pulling carts equipped with large rubber wheels, carrying supplies to the various units of the 2nd Battalion.

The head of the convoy was a 'mule-soldier', a real one. He can speak to his animals, we feel that he loves them. As for the men, it is not much fun. Right away we have the anticipation of trouble to come. Two artillery barrages ahead: "It's set like clockwork in the same place. When it starts next to you, you have not even heard the real shooting. It's like that with this gun shit. Anyway, when it comes you forget everything! That's what happened to a poor convoy last week. The mules were the only ones who survived in three months of this shit!"

The man explains the 'promenade'. The carts are kept at a distance of fifty yards from each other. Two or three soldiers walk alongside each cart. At some points we are exposed. You have to cross as fast as you can by pushing the carts with all your strength. He will give us the signal when this deadly race begins.

Making sure that men have understood, I distributed them between the carriages and we go, with the sound of distant artillery fire in the back. I walk with the first couple of soldiers alongside the head of the convoy. Suddenly, the mule leader

78

signals, we stop. The carriages move together. The mule leader points to the first corner where the famous hundred fifty yards had to be crossed without cover. There is just one way: run, run, run as fast as you can, run to escape, stay glued to the carriage, let the mule lead the way and know where to stop.

Who wants to go first? I accept. Final instructions to the two soldiers who accompany me. Load everything on the trolley, gun, ammunition, gas mask, food bag, and we only keep the helmet, "let's go".

Approaching the turn, the mule shows signs of nervousness. He trots faster. The mule leader launches his signal. Now. I'm praying. We rush forward, running, pushing the vehicle, running. Behind us, before us, artillery rounds fall everywhere. Whistles, explosions. With incredible energy the mules manage to gallop. We scramble, stumble, fall into the dust. I scream: "Get up! Forward!" Out of breath, we stop. That's it, we find ourselves unharmed. The mule is waiting quietly, his leader quietly finishing a cigarette.

In Russia, I had become acquainted with the famous 'Stalin's organs', the cluster rocket artillery. Their shots were fairly accurate but their whistling announced their coming and we could take cover. Here, no time for that. My two soldiers were in shock after their 'baptism of fire'.

The other three carts were not so lucky: one of my men wounded in the back and leg, a cart had two destroyed tires and the barrels of soup cracked. The wounds of my soldier did not seem too serious. I gave him a makeshift bandage while the mule leader cared for his beasts. Three teams were safe. There remained the fourth that was slow in coming, while artillery rounds exploded all over again and again. I decide to go alone to meet that team but the mule leader advises me to wait a little longer, "This is certainly a trick of the old ..." It seems that the age of the soldiers had not nothing to do with ordinary time: the 'old one' in question, head mule leader, is perhaps 23 or 24 years old! He was experienced, brave, and had a long year in Russia to his credit.

Indeed, a few minutes later, he crossed the free fire zone. Without taking any break, the 'old' rushed the mule so much that it hurt to see it. Then he notes the damage on the carriages. He is angry with rage: "If I find that bastard, I'll strangle him with my own hands!" "What a bastard!" "Who is the spy! Who directs the artillery fire!" For two weeks, things had not changed, the shots are not random. They only shoot when the convoy passes. The mule chief is furious. I imagine that if the Americans do not destroy the road from the sea it is certainly their intention to do so soon.

Second pass: two hundred yards, short of breath, closely followed by death. We pass without damage. In a clear sky, the rising moon allows us to distinguish Mount Scauri. We have arrived. The Battalion staff is installed in a large house hidden from sight by large trees. They thank our carriers. They do not linger. They wrap some kind of shoes around the legs of their animals and then leave in the silence of that night.

How delightful this night could be in peacetime, this Mediterranean night, lit by a round moon, and this silence! The same calm in times of war engendered anxiety. When? How? Where will the sound and fury be unleashed? The question haunts us. To forget, each is absorbing himself in his tasks.

They direct me to the 4th howitzers company. Its leader, Captain Vetter receives me happily. Reinforcements! He intends to give me the advanced observation group on Mount Scauri. The head of this post and a soldier have been killed. "Pure carelessness!" says Vetter. "These men have ignored the many warnings of their leaders. They probably left their daytime job to respond to a 'call of nature', and that was enough to signal their presence to the enemy. Our opponents do not just observe. What they want is to destroy our positions. They want to make us 'blind'. What good would our howitzers do if we have no one to direct fire? Just go for the protection of the rock when their battery of cannons start firing on the observation station."

This is what has just happened. Rule number one: absolute support, report any exceptional moves. Then he hammers his fist on the table: "During the day there is no standing down! Your new observation post is better protected with better visibility. The equipment is improved. Last night, telescopic binoculars have been installed, with telephone, radio and an experienced observer, Corporal Schmidt, a good soldier. Two good men are part of your group together with six sharp shooters. They must prevent possible infiltration by enemy commandos."

Before he had time to indicate the positions on the map, a shell exploded near the camp. Vetter was in a rage: "It's always those spies, just as the chief mule driver said. It was the same schedule of shelling and the same targets, and the shots are always accurate. Vetter showed us his plans regarding the Canadian soldiers facing us. Two weeks ago, one of their patrol was surprised as they landed their craft in a small cove where the Italian resistance was waiting for them. Ignoring earlier warning by the resistance the Canadians were spoiling for a fight. They unleashed a heavy barrage of fire in their attempt to get back to sea but their boat was destroyed. Four survivors of the commando were captured besides their Italian guide. The capture of these men allowed the dismantling of a spy network. The Canadians also provided their share of information telling us about their imminent major offensive. It also explained the relative calm on the Monte Cassino front. In the short term, concluded Vetter, the problem remains with the Italian spies who direct artillery fire against us.

From our vantage point, the following days went by smoothly. We remained hidden during the day because the Allied fighter bombers and their spy planes were constantly taking pictures of our positions, shooting at anything that moved. Their trucks were rolling day and night without being in the least disturbed by us. The area around Monte Cassino received intermittent exchanges of gunfire but no massive bombing. Still there was the obsessive certainty that something terrible was about to happen.

Starting May 10, things accelerated. That morning, as I returned from my night duties, our company commander urgently invited me to have coffee with other section heads. He quickly came to the point: the German General Staff was convinced that the Allies will launch their offensive any day now. They will seek to break our lines of defense to march on Rome. Two possibilities: first, they might attack by the seaside highway, second, the plain of Cassino-Pontecorvo defended by our paratroopers. It is imperative to strengthen the protection of our howitzers and double the number of shells. From tonight, there is maximum alert. I have to take the observation post for three nights and probably also during the day in case the offensive was launched in the morning. I have to place a second phone line with a second team. Both positions will be covered but I am the only one in touch with the base. I have to arrange everything for the next three days and especially: "Do not forget: without you, we are blind! Good luck!"

The two observation posts are set. The first high alert night is just as the others with the highlight being the arrival of the 'soup carrier'. Eight people to feed, two observers, six shooters. Every night, it was the turn of a different soldier to perform this chore. He must be very fast without spilling the precious food. The rest of the night passed listening to the constant parade of Allied trucks at a distance. For the first time, the sound of the chains of armored vehicles is heard. I phone my report.

The only thing left is to wait. The soldier who accompanies me is called Ekkard. I ask him to tell me a little about himself. I believed he expected this after three days with me! He immediately inundates me with a flood of personal stories. He has two boys who are fifteen and sixteen ready to fight for the Führer and Fatherland. He was a bank manager in Magdeburg. The city was bombed and destroyed. That's why he volunteered to follow the Führer in his total war until the final victory. He was a real fanatic! Caution ... I commend him: "Bravo Ekkard! It's time to participate in his final glorious victory!" Obviously unable to suspect any irony on my part he replied: "Ah! You know about our Fuehrer's secret weapons? When the Führer gives the order, England will be razed, including all their troops and all the allied armies. The Eastern Front will fall to our new weapons and we'll be the victors of a new world. We have suffered enough by the injustice of the world. Revenge will be terrible."

He doesn't let loose: "I saw you pray several times, I think it was for our final victory. I do not believe anything because I feel like the Führer that religion is the opium of the people, and I'm against any drugs."

I replied without hesitation:"If I pray it is that God may protect us and that we can find our families unharmed. Imagine that I included you in my prayers because I think we will need the most of God's protection in the coming days, perhaps even in the next hours." He looks at me with an air of arrogance and perhaps I seem strange to him, but perhaps a little less so. According to his rank he must obey me but I cannot treat him like a common soldier, he is 44 years old, he could be my father. Other than his fanatism he is an intelligent and cultivated person. Ekkard impressed me by his experience with banking, his erudition, and his knowledge of Greco-Roman mythology.

The front was quiet, too quiet. At 3pm, as usual, we lower the telescopic binoculars to avoid sun glare. My soldiers and I can sleep in turns.

As evening fell, an awful weariness came over me, followed by panic. I am sure: the next few hours are going to be terrible. It's time to make my report to the company commander. At 6pm, soldier Schmidt called me to the first aid station: soup arrived. Already? "Yes, today the mule trip went quietly, no shots."

I send Ekkard to get our ration. The sky is cloudy but with the full moon I can faintly distinguish my surroundings. I see nothing coming, not a single truck or a sound. Castelforte to one side and Monte Cassino to the other, nothing more. It feels as quiet and scary as in a fantastic movie. Two armies that betray nothing of their presence are yet definitely there melded into the landscape ready to tear each other apart. I choke. Anxiety tied my bowels.

Ekkard returns full of energy. For him, everything goes well, he welcomes the very nice evening 'menu' and wishes me good appetite, "Look! We even have a true Pilsen, a rice substitute, with fresh meat (I thought of our wounded mules) and even white bread with a piece of cheese!"

Indeed, it is unusually good, a royal dinner. To me, it was the meal of the condemned! I take a sip of beer but otherwise I can't eat. Impossible, I am a total prisoner of fear. It is almost midnight, I need to breathe! I take hold of myself to call Captain Vetter. He is not mincing words: "Yes, I believe the time has arrived now. At midnight they will bury us under bombs and at dawn tomorrow they will attack with tanks and infantry." I listen carefully as he continues with instructions and look at my watch: midnight. At that moment, the enemy attack came, it is the worst I have ever experienced, a vision forever etched in my mind. It is May 11, 1944.

In a flash, the whole coastal strip turns into a giant eruption of fire spewing a flood of steel in a titanic din on us. We are literally paralyzed, unable to form a thought. As a final gesture I put the phone away under a rock and downed the telescopic binoculars. Around us the earth shook with convulsive tremors, everything is but a vast blaze. It is death dancing in fury above our heads. Surely our last hour has arrived. So, knees on the ground, all that remains is to pray to God to forgive me. "Holy Virgin pray for us and protect us!"

How long did I pray? How long have I implored the grace and help of God? Such moments are not measured in human minutes. One enters another dimension. I felt a presence enter me like I distinctly heard someone say, "Do not worry, I'm here!" My body and mind are one, I am at peace, free from fear. A great sense of relief comes over me. Nothing can touch me, all in my fervor for God: "Our Father who art in heaven, Your will be done......"

From that day, I knew that the only freedom that matters is not to fear death. Words will forever fail to describe the revelation of that terrible night. All I can say is that faith in God as I had maintained until then was little compared to my new certainty. Since that night I know that God is truly with us!

Full of great happiness I'm back down to earth! My companion Ekkart is on the ground, trembling and moaning And now it was he who asked me to help him pray! I rebound. Suddenly, I am aware that we have not put on our helmets! By threading my own, I yell at Ekkard: "Quick, your helmet!" A shell exploded a few yards from our rock. A tremendous blow stuns me. I do not hear the screaming, crying and moaning. A terrible head pain prevents me from getting up. Ekkard comes to help me, thanking the sky and I manage to sit. Blood is running down my face. Shrapnel pierced my helmet. Then, with infinite precautions and difficulties, I remove my headphones. Ekkard cannot believe it. He keeps mumbling, "Thank God he's alive. Ten seconds earlier, you would have been dead! Always keep a good relationship with your guardian angel."

The artillery fire had demolished all of our positions. It was now more than 2am. I tried to use the phone line to call the first aid station, nothing. Silence. I order Ekkard and Schmidt to repair the lines and then ordered them to withdraw to our gathering point at the command post of our company before dawn.

Left alone in my position, I back up the telescopic binoculars to resume surveying the field. Their artillery is now focusing on our rear positions, our fortifications and our artillery in their mountain positions. At 3am, Ekkard resurfaces, livid: "The aid station behind us was hit hard." "And Schmidt?" He and his companion were shredded by the blast, and our gear and ammunition pulverized. As to the monitoring station, it was abandoned. In sum, there remains only one man behind us and two supervisors. The battery of howitzers is no longer useful. In these circumstances, it is better to withdraw immediately or send a messenger to the company to take orders.

No time to think as phosphorous bombs raining down on the trees set them ablaze at once, releasing a thick smoke. Gas masks! Quick! Already there is another threat, this time from the sea, a hissing roar, a deafening roar that passes over our heads and leaves a path of death and destruction in what is left of our defense lines. Suddenly I understood. The phosphorus bombs have transformed our peninsula into a sign post that they use to guide the shooting of the Allied navy anchored in the Gulf of Gaeta. The smoke dissipated, I take off my mask. From Scauri, Castelforte all the way to Monte Cassino, everywhere, all the way, vegetation blazes. How can there be any survivors after such an inferno?

With my telescopic binoculars, thanks to the full moon, I can see hundreds and hundreds of armored vehicles on the roads ahead. The ground assault is imminent. "Ekkard! Come and see! Look through the binoculars, and just ahead, you will see your Führers' 'secret weapon'! Come on! Look!" He does not come. He has collapsed, totally disoriented. He no longer has the strength to mumble. In the fire of this corner of Italy, his entire worldview is about to go up in smoke. He no longer believes in secret weapons, nor of ideology, nor Hitler. He thinks of his sons. What will they become?

"Ekkard! Come!" Even in a panic, I wanted him to live. To pull rank? It was not very clear in my mind. In the German army, it was not allowed for superiors to fraternize with simple soldiers.

As the navy ships stop their shelling, tanks enter the scene. Battle rages in front and around Scauri and nearby Minturno. This indicates that our first defense lines were breached and annihilated. For us, only one solution: clear out quickly without being noticed. Three of our soldiers have joined us. The descent of the hill offered an unimaginable spectacle: an armada of warships occupies the Gulf of Gaeta. "Look, Ekkard, that's the American superpower. There are no material limits for them! Look at the sky, there, hundreds of bombers will squash what remains of our troops around Monte Cassino. Where are our planes, our fighters, our submarines, our secret weapons? Where? Ekkard, we're screwed! I do not want to die for your Greater Germany! I want to see my parents again! Look, Ekkard on our belt buckles is engraved 'God with us'. This is blasphemy! We will be severely punished for our hybris. I never hurt anyone, but still I obey a diabolical power that sows terror and death in Europe! Every day I beg the indulgence of God to forgive us and that He keeps us under the protection of His love."

My last words are lost in the din of the fighter-bombers. We are their game, their 'German game'. Luckily, we reached an orchard that offer us protection. Now it's daytime. We steal our way through the trees towards our company. A soldier appeared and motioned to approach. I'm going to meet him. He presents himself: Corporal Dropp. He has the expected orders for us. Our battalion was forced to retreat to Formia. The company is leaving around 4am.

The front moved so quickly that our little group now finds itself behind the Allied's lines. The German defense was shattered: burnt out armored vehicles all the way to Formia. I tell my men, "We will move forward in the direction of Formia, always away from the road under the cover of trees. Before Formia, we will cross the road into the mountains to get around the city. On the other side, we will find our battalion. Following the plan, our division has to take position at the entrance of the valley to defend the road to Itri where we may meet with Italian resistance. Everything must be done to avoid them. Dropp, if something happens to me, take command. We leave in single file, follow me, and you, Dropp, you bring up the rear."

We advance on tiptoe. We hear tanks plying the road, while the planes fly over us relentlessly. Surely the aircraft carriers on the Gulf of Gaeta are their base. On the road, a wave of panic: what remained of our artillery is hitting back. Several vehicles burn or explode. Allied armored vehicles seek refuge on the sides of the road. We turn back into hiding but soon our artillery is silent. Their response lasted only twenty minutes, however, enough to disrupt the Allied columns. For our troops it is a life saver, at least we have an opportunity to regroup.

A meager margin for maneuver indeed.

The enemy movements do not point towards the sea but were concentrated along the Scauri-Formia Road. We are, therefore, behind the front. The sun was beating down. Even though we are hungry and thirsty we wanted to avoid isolated farms, yet it was the only place where maybe we would find food. I weighed the pros and cons if we were caught face to face with the farmers or the Italian resistance. Perhaps in the din of gunfire we could pass unnoticed. More than anything, we were afraid of being spotted.

I decide to take the risk of exposing my men to this dangerous business. We now cross vineyards where airplanes could see us. Our helmets were changed for our caps, adorned by vine branches. Camouflage. Five hundred yards ahead, I saw a big farmhouse surrounded by trees. I tell Dropp that I will go on reconnaissance. He follows me from afar with binoculars and monitors the surroundings.

Passing stealthily through the grapevine I remember the not so distant days of my boy scout treasure hunts? The truth is that I hoped I would not be surprised! Grove after grove, I approach. Nothing. I walk a little more, I trick by throwing stones, left, right, center. Nothing. No reaction. I now distinguish the farm buildings and its grand entrance. I walk up inside the courtyard. Stupor! There is a tank. No one notices anything. This is an enemy armor! I walk around the buildings. No guard. To the right, I hear laughter and loud voices. They are speaking English.

I turned back to join the group. I tell them that there are ways to get food. "Comrades, we will simply say hello to those soldiers, disarm them, put them in a corner and take their place at the table. Wonderful, isn't it?"

Silence. My enthusiasm is hardly returned. Ekkard glances at my bandaged head. No! I'm not delirious, I distributed the roles: "Ekkard, you speak English, you stay with me. Dropp, with three men, stand at the entrance well hidden. With Ekkard, I want to surprise the tank crew. When we cry 'Hands up!' you blast in shouting 'Hurrah!' Take two hand grenades and get ready to launch if we fail. Everything clear? Let's go!"

Ekkard and I get into a shed by a back door. The place was full of large tractors and other agricultural equipment. Through the windows we see the huge signs on the sides of the tank in the colors of the Canadian army. "Let's go through the inside. It is too risky from the outside." We find a door connecting the shed and the house. Our intention is not to kill. Noiselessly, we arrive in the open courtyard and like devils in a box we surge against the Canadians. "Hands up!" The five Canadians were against the wall. Then with a "Hurrah!" Drop and his team followed as expected. The Canadians do not budge. They just look at us with curiosity.

These are great fellows, beefy, full of life. I ask Dropp to disarm them. One of them had a pistol and two machine guns were hanging near the door. "Ekkard, monitor our prisoners with three men. Dropp, check whether there are any Canadians still in the tank." Dropp emerges from the tank brandishing cigarette packets, cans, two loaves, chocolate. It's like Christmas on the 1st of May!

Back in the dining room, I find Ekkard in conversation with the commander of the tank. Our five Canadians are still sitting quietly against the wall. They are watching us curiously, no hostility in their eyes. They are all older than I, perhaps between 24 and 28 years. Ekkard translated the story of their adventure. They left the road when our artillery opened fire. Chance led them to the deserted house where they decided to quietly wait out the shelling. They settled in, having unearthed a well stocked cellar. They had not even seen fit to install a guard post.

- Is the commander an officer?

- Yes, a lieutenant, 28, active military.

It's almost 6pm and I calculate that we are four miles from Formia. It is essential to move out together and find a way to cross the road without being noticed. To try to join our unit dragging our prisoners behind us does not make sense. Strictly speaking, one could use them as 'hostages' to cross the road where we would release them. We could also eliminate them altogether. This was not an option, I fundamentally rejected it. Ekkard seems to await my orders.

- Yes, Ekkard, we are at war and in a delicate position. How to part with our prisoners without putting us in danger? You know my moral and Christian beliefs: I never kill a prisoner or an unarmed man. And you, Ekkard?

- Be assured, I don't either. I have only one desire: to see my family as soon as possible.

- You, Dropp?

- Me, too!

Ekkard takes the initiative: "Let me do it. Their commander is a good guy, I will make a gentleman's agreement with him, on soldier's honor. They will accompany us to the road where we will give them their freedom, provided they lead us through safely." This is a solution that suits me fine. Ekkard, go tell them. Somehow I feel that something is wrong. I ask Ekkard to translate: "The Canadian officer just explained to me that they are not at all worried. Even if we would not release them, they know they will be free before nightfall. He also said that we have very little chance of crossing the busy road, let alone the front line. He said that our army will not have the time to regroup or build new defenses."

I was not about to give up on my proposal. I wanted to scare the Canadians into doing what I wanted. I asked Ekkard to tell their commander: "You took refuge in this farm far away from the battlefield to spend the night in safety and to wait quietly until you felt safe to rejoin your unit. In our army this attitude has a name: desertion in the face of the enemy. Accordingly, you would be courtmartialed. You are our prisoners and you can imagine that we could neutralize you for eternity, not to be seen nor heard by anyone."

The Canadians remain unmoved. I continue: "We are soldiers, not killers. What matters to us is to rejoin our company. You're right to say that crossing the road and the front will be difficult. So I think we're going back and look for a good place to cross the lines. You will find a way to make it possible for us to cross the road. I think you are men of honor. Let us find a solution to the best of our mutual interests."

My words seemed to have had an effect. The Canadian commander asked one of his men to respond. Surprise! This soldier speaks German! He has followed all our discussions and reported them to his officer all along. As we had requested the officer agrees that we turn back together.

After walking five hundred yards, we are at the road. A convoy of Allied trucks is passing in front of us. Accompanied by one of his men, the Canadian commander plans to intercept the convoy at the next turn, giving us a chance to quickly cross the road. He cannot stand on the road without weapons, nor the man accompanying him. This will seem too suspect. He is right. I ask Dropp to return their weapons. He receives them calmly. Then he holds out his hand: "We have concluded a peace between soldiers. You risk nothing from us. It's time to go fast! The night begins to fall and the moon is not up yet."

Outside, relative calm returned. On the road, you can hear the trucks but they drive more slowly. I walk ahead with the Canadian officer. The others follow Dropp and this unusual German-Canadian column. We're almost there. "The turn is fifty yards ahead. I'll go with a soldier. You go just around the bend without being noticed. You hide there and wait for my signal to cross."

In the shadows, we wait. Three or four trucks pass, then nothing. This is the time: "Go ahead! Go fast! Good luck!" Crossing the road at full speed, racing breathlessly between vineyards before collapsing to the ground. Everyone agrees that what just happened with Canadians is incredible. Ekkard recalls that during the First World War, some of the agreements took place between enemies, for example at the Christmas cease fires. Whatever!

We managed to cross this cursed road and that was the main thing!

According to my calculations we were five miles from Formia. We had to head for the mountains and pass the front line far enough from the city: "Go! Right now!"

In the bright moon light, we advanced without much trouble. Small arms fire was focused on the city and its surroundings. After gaining the miles, I feel it is time to give my men a break. A group of large trees will shelter us. This position was easy to find because after the meal I intended to leave with Ekkard for reconnaissance. All was quiet.

With Ekkard at my side I walk towards Formia but soon ahead, engine noise announced the arrival of heavy vehicles. We quickly hide. As we walk further, we discover the intentions of the Allied. They prepared for the attack the next day, bypassing Formia, heading for the city of Itri. It is time for us to move to the other side.

Upon our return to my men we leave for Itri. Hours of walking. We must also avoid being caught by the German military police who would incorporate us automatically in the Formia defense units. Here we are, finally, at Itri. We meet many dispersed German troops. A chaos. Once in the city, I start looking for information. I learned that our regiment is stationed on the other side of Itri, ready to go to Frosinone. It would be really a mistake to miss them being so close! In a fast move we catch our company just before it vacates its position.

When he saw us Captain Vetter was flabbergasted. Between amazement and joy, tears came to his eyes: "I had put a cross on you! I lost over half my men, not to mention our hardware. The third section, with Lieutenant Weber, on the way to Scauri ... Three howitzers, eighteen men ... Everything was pulverized ... Not a single survivor! Our division has lost 70% of its force. We have orders to fall back urgently to Frosinone. The Allies have pierced the front of Pontecorvo. Monte Cassino fell and tomorrow if we do not manage to cross the plain to the mountains we will be cut off and surrounded unless there is a miracle, a reinforcement of armored and artillery, and our troops manage to delay the Allied advance to Rome." I wanted to make my report but Vetter did not let me continue: "It's good, it's good, the main thing is that you are here."

- Tomorrow defending Formia?

A battalion of the 11 th Division had the formal order to delay the advance of the Allies at any cost. This is a like a death sentence, they will all be spent at Itri. There is a second line of defense, plus another battalion of the 11th because it is essential to stop the enemy. We learned a few days later that the defenders of Formia fought a fierce battle throughout the day, crushed by the bombarding of the Navy. Some survivors were taken prisoner. As for the Itri line of defense, it held its position for three days before being destroyed too. Thanks to these brave fighters, a large part of the German troops could escape to the mountains and secure the roads leading to the center of Italy, to Tivoli, Rieti and other sectors.

Along these roads, day after day, we had to suffer attacks by fighter-bombers, leaving us with very few men. After Tivoli, we received the order to create a new line of defense. The group of men under my command had been restructured. The 'old' team was still there. Ekkard and Dropp with me joined by two new soldiers, specially trained in the use of a heavy machine gun. We had to take position on a hill overlooking the road to Rieti with the sole aim to slow the progress of the Americans.

Off we went with two machine guns, model 42, very fast shooting but huge consumers of ammunition. Every man is responsible for two ammunition supply crates. Once on the hill, I install both MGs, five hundred yards apart. I place Ekkard and a comrade between firing positions to serve as liaison position and Dropp responsibility for the gun to my right. The main thrust of our defense is to never use two guns simultaneously. I also emphasize the camouflage. Final recommendation to my men: "Always look at the sky. Our number one enemy is the spy plane. It flies very slowly, often at very low altitude. He would see a mouse in the grass! So beware! Currently, the road is free, no

Americans in sight. We will focus the turn of the road in front of us, at 500-600 yards, firing on all vehicles except armored. When the troops retreat behind the bend cease fire. Wait until I resume firing. For the rest, say a prayer, the day will be tough. May God protect us."

We are now in full daylight. It's time for a snack. During the day, we perhaps will not have the opportunity. For Americans, this road is a must. It runs along the side of the mountain. From where we are, it's easy to target motor vehicles. American soldiers are accustomed to move only in the wake of armor.

At 7pm, the fighter-bombers fly overhead and start pounding the positions in the back of us. Immediately, armored vehicles are in sight. They stop before the turn and then one of them advances alone. He has hardly reached the middle of the turn, when two cannon shots reach them in full force. These shots came from our howitzers from a dug-in position, beginning to harrass the road. The American response team does not wait. Their artillery and airplanes come in. We stay quiet for now, they have not spotted us. Meanwhile a heavy US vehicle has cleared the road of the burned out tank throwing the debris into the ravine.

Soon, thirty tanks swoop down on the road. In their wake, the first infantry vehicles pass the turn. As agreed with Dropp, my station then opened fire, supported effectively by our howitzers setting a light armored vehicle immediately in flames. The road is impassable again. The infantry was down behind the curve, leaving it to aviation and artillery to clear the ground. We are spotted and the famous cannon batteries bombard us for ten minutes. Hell! When the shelling stops two fighter planes fly over our hill several times. They are mostly interested in our howitzers. They attack, while the Americans move to reach the road again. A vehicle passes the tanks, accompanied by the infantry. We must react. On Dropp's side, total silence. I send Ekkard for news while I take to strafing their vehicles. Without the support of our artillery, I order a cease fire and to retreat behind the protection of some large rocks. It was just in time! The fighter planes are back and this time it is our positions they have in their crosshairs. They strafe the hill before disappearing but our refuge is well protected. I sent two soldiers to recover the guns and decide to join Dropp but when I arrive, I see Ekkard is defeated. At his side, the other liaison soldier cries. It is clear, Dropp has died.

I approach cautiouly. How awful! Dropp is almost cut in half, he certainly died instantly. The other two soldiers lay near him. How awful! My God, how horrible! I'm in shock, incapable of any decision. Nothing left to do but pray, "Lord have mercy, Lord grant them eternal peace. Lord, give them peace, they have not had time to ask you. Amen." A great calm came over me. Should it take a horrible fate to find the love and tenderness of God?

No time for fussing. A spy plane flies over our positions. Then I see him slowly approach our group. He flies so low that I clearly distinguished the pilot's face. It is to him that I address myself. I put the bodies of my comrades in his sight with a helpless gesture, accompanied by a sign of the cross. I hope he would understand our situation, the universal dismay at death. The plane made a U-turn, he rolls over us so low that I can share an intense look with the pilot. He finally flies away. For Ekkard, the case is clear: we will be bombed. I am convinced that he is mistaken. Something tells me this flier understood my silent message: "No, Ekkard, we now have the time to look after our dead."

We need stretchers and help. I send a soldier. An hour later, he returns empty-handed. He found not a soul. The artillery barrage moved away from us. We are behind enemy lines! With improvised stretchers we transport the bodies to the bottom of the hill on a rough path that makes it a real ordeal for an appalling funeral. Below is a seemingly deserted village destroyed by the bombing. We are exhausted but I find the energy to go around the houses and in a garden I discovered six fresh graves - some macabre type of luck in all our misfortune. It is in this forgotten corner of Italy where we burried our comrades. There they rest forever, crude crosses on their graves, and a simple piece of paper attached to them bearing their names, the designation of their company, battalion and division. We prayed for a long time at the graves and recited the "Our Father...". Ekkard started the German military funeral song, a very moving tribute to our fallen comrades. When I say "sing" we sang out loud as if to let the whole world know our sorrow, our broken heart, with tears in our eyes. We were totally absorbed by this funeral. We no longer belonged to the world. We no longer hear anything. When I turned around, there was an American patrol, their guns raised at us. I did not resist and tell my men: "Let's raise our hands, we are prisoners."

At my request, Ekkard explains to the Americans why we are here. As he speaks, two soldiers disarm us. That was what the spy plane had done - sent the order to capture us. In reality, they had been watching us ever since our arrival in the village. They were moved by our attitude and our grief and that's why they delayed the time of our capture. In short, they showed pity and humanity.

Nonetheless, we are now prisoners. In my bag I have the identification papers and personal belongings of my three fallen comrades. How to send them to their families? I thought about it while we were driven to a make shift POW camp.

There we find a hundred other prisoners. Ekkard is following me. In this day of reckoning, he wants to confide in me: "For us, the war is over. Perhaps we will stay together, at least for some time. Anyway, I hope. Now you are no longer my boss but I have great respect for your courage, your sense of responsibility and the way you always remained human. At my age, I thought I knew everything. It took me two weeks of real war and three weeks with you to realize that I was wrong. Thank you, my friend, yes, thank you with all my heart."

Since I also hoped we would stay together, I thanked him. Anyway, I'm not worried about him, his knowledge of English would make him useful. For me, the decision was made. At the first opportunity, I will escape from this camp, I would find my battalion and my comrades! We retreated from the enemy but we will rejoin our side.

Rumors floated around of an imminent landing by the Allied in northern France. Italy might be evacuated by our troops in a few months and the war would end. For me it meant only one thing: by the end of the year, I'll be home. This hoped for sequence of events appeared to me as obvious, I had not the slightest desire to rot here, and spend perhaps years as a prisoner of war. This time, despite my good relationship with Heaven, I did not know what my future would hold for me. Otherwise, I would quietly remain in American hands unless new events would again change my 'life plan'.

I did not say goodbye to my friend Ekkard. I just moved along as if I had nothing on my mind, leaving him in a long discussion with three other soldiers. I went around in the crowd of prisoners in search of useful information. Just for the unlikely chance to find others from my batallion I shouted out loud the name of our battalion, looking for some prisoners who might go with me.

Two men responded. We introduced ourselves. One was a staff corporal of our company. He told me about the happenings of the last few days, that the Americans had captured them not far from the road and that our company had suffered heavy losses. Finally, the battalion had to retreat to avoid encirclement. He told me that a column of prisoners is already scheduled to leave this camp and others will soon follow. Americans are waiting with trucks to take everybody to Naples and from there to the United States! True or false, this information is most helpful to plan my escape. I had no desire to go to America in such conditions! The camp's security does not seem to be a priority for our captors. They probably thought that no one in his right mind would want to get back to the slaughter of the battle. So I approach two American soldiers who are supposed to guard us and ask if I could go to take care of my 'needs' in the vineyards. OK, no problem, go right ahead. They let me get away! Under the cover of the vineyard I run away at full speed.

The night was almost black. Racing between the vines, my face and hands were scratched and bleeding. Behind me everything remained calm. My absence had apparently not been noticed. So I slowed my pace and started looking to orient myself. Far away you could hear gunfire but in front of me, no noise. I had to save my energies. To keep walking in these conditions was to risky. I looked for shelter under a tree to rest and to wait for morning. Aircraft noise woke me up. I had slept in an orchard. Everywhere cherries, peaches, apples. It was close to neighboring houses. Extreme caution, avoid meeting and try at all costs to move on. I selected a big tree and I climbed. To the West in the plain, a road, probably the one that connects to Tivoli and Rieti. Behind me close by, mountains still flushed by sunrise. I pick some fruit and take the direction to the mountains, with the intention of going northwards.

On the third day I got the distinct feeling that I was getting closer to the front lines. Our troops must have offered severe resistance judging by the incessant attacks of the fighter-bombers. This made me leave the mountains so I could move faster. Towards evening there is the sound of small arms fire. Lost in thought I hear an order in German in the back of me: "Hands up! Who are you?" They were Germans! A sergeant and three soldiers point their guns at me. They seem very suspicious and searched me while I keep my hands up. I explained my situation to the sergeant, "Okay, I believe you, but come with us, you will explain it all to our superiors. We are a reconnaissance patrol. We are looking for Italian resistance fighters. Dressed in German army uniforms they attacked one of our convoys this morning."

A surprise awaits me. The head of the company is none other than my Captain Vetter! Where is it written that I should always follow him, and he me! I hasten to give him a report, and we leave together. Along the way, Vetter makes me aware of the latest disaster: "Our regiment is completely dislocated, many captured, the other on the run. Our howitzer company no longer exists. There are no more howitzers. Finished. For now, we expect some trucks to get here on the back roads bringing some food, we hope.

Then we set off again at night through the mountains around Rieti before daybreak."

*

On June 5, 1944, near Perugia, my Italian campaign was nearing its end. Our battalion was just a group of routed soldiers. The term 'offensive' was no longer part of our vocabulary, except to describe the action of the Allied. For a long time our actions were aimed only to defend, always defend.

With a group of ten men and three guns, we had taken a position on the crest of a steep hill. Exhausted, we came to grips with this terrible reality before dark. Our three fire stations are installed. A soldier stays with me to connect with the rest of the company, which is reduced to sixty men stationed at a shelter two hundred meters below. They must have some rest. My group also must rest since fatigue and extreme exhaustion crush even the most valiant soldiers. I give the order to get short periods of sleep in turn. In principle, we do not risk much. It seems that the enemy will attack in the morning by road and by plane, in the usual way. Consequence of these predictions: Again our staff has focused our defense on the heights overlooking the road. Nothing new in this strategy. However, while inspecting our firing positions, I think that a good Indian chief would choose the difficult terrain to sneak behind our lines and sow panic. My word! Am I playing cowboys and Indians or what? I laugh to myself. Still, I remind everyone: utmost caution.

After these instructions, I moved to the central firing station. We are four men and we let the two gunners sleep. They collapse immediately. I settled myself next to the machine gun and also succumb to sleep. A nightmare wakes me up with a start: the noise of stones tumbling down the hill. I'm scanning the darkness, nothing abnormal. My team is sleeping. I wake up my neighbor, the sharpshooter, putting my hand over his mouth. Signing to him I make him understand that there is a strange commotion ahead.

He moved immediately behind his machine gun and I send my urgent message to the company commander: "We have visitors. We must put the battalion on alert." The night is gray. I scrutinizes the darkness, frightened at the thought that the two other positions might be asleep, they may already be neutralized. A quick response is required. I give an order to my machine gun man: "I'll throw a hand grenade as far as I can. Once it explodes, you spray all the ground before us."

The grenade explodes, our machine gun spits fire. The second rifle man starts screaming. He seems to have lost his head. The right machine gun is also beginning to crackle. Left, no reaction. Grenades explode, but they are now coming from the others. Before us, shadows advance, men who shoot at us. We return their fire. The enemy is surprised. He backs up. To our left, he has pierced our defenses. The post to my right continues to defend well. The attack on the two positions is repelled but my left is immobilized. I suppose our company launched a counter-attack.

Suddenly the night lights up with rocket flares. Artillery showers us with shells of all calibers. A spy plane turns above us. We will be reduced to dust. Holy Virgin, protect us! The spy plane directs the fight to the rear, where our battalion is located. That gives us the opportunity to go. I ask my two men to take the machine gun and ammunition. We leave! No answer. To the right the shooting resumed. Who is doing the shooting? Ours? Others? Total confusion, absolute panic. I lean toward my rifle man. He lies next to his machine, half the face torn off. The machine gun? Out of commission. My second man took refuge behind a rock. His body is only a single huge wound dripping blood. I load him on my back and walk into the night hoping to find help. The man groans and then is silent. I collapse under his weight, I'm covered in blood, my back is soaked. My God, do not let him die! Give me the strength to save him. I call with all my strength amid the uproar. I am desperate. Behind me, someone down the slope, screaming and crying. I shouted to him: "come here!" It's the youngest of my soldiers, from the right post.

"They're after me!" he screams. "So come, we will take our comrade with us." Too late. As I start to climb I see that he is dead. In a few hurried moves I take his identification plate, recover what I find in his pockets and we flee, after throwing a last grenade far back.

In the back, we hear a firefight. Ours repelling the enemy? As if pushed by an invisible hand, I continue to run backwards, with my young soldier at my side. Lying on the ground, slowly we catch our breath and realize that we are deserting our unit! Behind us, there is a hard fight going on while we flee for our lives. My young companion stares at me with the look of a dog that expects everything from his master. This is terrible!

It is plain daylight now and this damn spy plane keeps circling above us like a vulture. This time, no luck for him. A burst of machine gun fire reaches him, it catches fire and crashes into our lines. This does not prevent the fighter planes to strafe and bomb us relentlessly. We continue our crazy race. German fighters just killed two of them, they are crashing down and barely missing us. On the road, we find our armored trucks taking position. This time, the Americans will have trouble piercing our lines!

This was the last thought I remember crossing my mind. Then I heard a terrible explosion. Then nothing.

When I regained consciousness, I was in a field hospital. Someone said, "The Allied landed in Normandy."

It was June 6, 1944.

*

Chapter 6

A New Front to Fight: the Gestapo

The Americans continued their advance and our army retreats. After four days in the field hospital, we are evacuated at night, twelve ambulances framed by an observation car and two jeeps. These vehicles were not armed. Their function was to check for hostile planes. To clearly show the nature of our convoy, a large Red Cross flag was deployed. We were the last to leave this small town north of Perugia.

The sun had just risen. In the sky, four fighter-bombers. Immediately, the jeeps alert the drivers of the ambulances to stop and to open the doors wide so that pilots can see that we were a transport for wounded. To our horror the convoy was targeted anyway and strafed from behind. Luckily, I'm in a front seat and an invisible hand pulls me out then nothing. I regain consciousness amid the screams of the wounded. The hand that had pushed me out of the ambulance now pulled me from the ditch. It is the driver.

Are you injured? Any deaths? Why has this aircraft shot at a convoy of ambulances? The driver listens to me without emotion. He sees that I, the sergeant, am clueless! "Fear not, the Americans are gone and I hope that the pilots realized their mistake. Come, lie down, I'll go to get information." I was shivering, my teeth chattering. A nurse passed by wondering if I have malaria. She covers me and gives me a shot. I fall asleep immediately.

The ambulance comes back and has to shake me awake. I'm always cold. He tells me that the last vehicle of the convoy was hit with a doctor inside. Half of all the ambulances were hit, two caught fire. We wait for another truck from the Red Cross. I offer my help. "You with your fever, stay here! Rest." Had I caught malaria? I fell back to sleep.

Again the ambulance comes to wake me up to give me the news: "Twenty-four deaths and serious injuries. A truck is loading the dead. In our ambulance, we have made room for one more casualty. He was in a car that burned."

The newcomer is lying right in front of me. I have a feeling he is trying to talk to me. Caution. He whispers to me: "You know, normally I would not have made it into this convoy, I was with you in the hospital for a malaria attack and under pressure from some Gestapo guy the doctor had issued the certificate that I had been cured. For me that meant back into battle. Your leaving at night was under so much confusion that I could slip into an ambulance by pretending to be injured. The doctor who had signed my papers was in the ambulance that was flattened. Now he is dead and I'm saved from the front for the moment. Once we are on the Red Cross boat the wounded will be operated on board and then possibly sent back to Germany. The boat is expected to leave early tomorrow morning for a port north of Rimini. Lets hope that the fighter-bombers will not come back."

Enough chatter! The nurse pricks our buttocks and we fall asleep. Night has fallen, ambulances are traveling at high speed, we are badly shaken but the injections plunge us into a semiconsciousness until we finally arrive at the Red Cross ship. Those who can walk are limping toward the boat, the others are carried on stretchers. When the transfer is made the ambulances leave at unbelievable speed. On the ship the dead are put into the hold, already cooled. The seriously injured go into the operating room, the other patients remain on the deck. The boat takes off to the North. Hardly on our way, first aid: changing dressings, taking temperature, all carefully noted on the chart that we carried around the neck ever since leaving the field hospital. A doctor examines me: 103°F. He asked the nurse about my wounds. Practically healed but not entirely. "Are you having a malaria attack?" An infernal noise interrupts. Six fighter-bombers flying over our ship, turn around and then resume altitude.

*

The stifling heat made me miserable all day. I prayed, I felt my end was near. They take me down to the malaria section, in the bottom hold. We finally dock in a port but not the planned one, and are taken to a Red Cross train. Too tired to ask questions I can only pray to the Good Lord to take me far, far away from Italy.

At the end of a seemingly interminable time I got the feeling that this train had carried us to heaven, the mountains were so high when we got off the train. We arrived at the Cortina d'Ampezzo ski resort! Everything was green, and neat, flowers everywhere. Buses and ambulances were waiting to take us to luxury hotels turned into hospitals.

Care continues, with more horrible quinine pills to swallow quickly, otherwise we would vomit as their taste was disgusting! The worst was the sudden bouts of fever, as much as 104°F. Blankets or not, teeth were chattering. Four patients per room, all suffering from malaria, a resident nurse to watch us. A doctor passed two or three times a day. We often passed out, completely drained by incredible spikes of fever. We slowly regained strength. The food was mostly in liquid form and of good quality. Above all, we were still alive!

Our nurses were very caring and very pretty! Their dialects revealed their origins: some from Austria, some German. The housekeepers were Italian, rather young and pretty. Everything was done to make our stay enjoyable. Was it so that we could be sent back to the front more quickly? Meanwhile, I thought I was in paradise. When we could get out of bed we walked down to the hotel restaurant in our striped gray and white pajamas. We had breakfast, lunch and dinner, always a buffet well stocked. At lunch and dinner we were entitled to a beer or a glass of wine.

A new doctor came by for an examination accompanied by a Gestapo man in uniform. This doctor's task was to determine whether the patients were ready to be sent back to the front. Looking me over he started to write on my chart that I would need at least three more weeks for recuperation. The Gestapo man looked at the chart and told the doctor to change his entry to say that I am ready to be sent to the front. The doctor said: "We cannot let him go in his condition." The Gestapo man started to yell: "This is my decision to make!" but after a heated discussion the Gestapo man angrily agreed: "Ok, give him another week, but no more, understand!" The doctor shrugged his shoulders and they left.

I was appalled about the callous ways of this Gestapo guy, and for showing his complete disregard for my need to gather the strength to get back into combat. After all, was I not one of the millions of soldiers who were doing all this fighting so that the likes of him could do their disgusting police work in great comfort and far from the front?

Later the nurse said: "This is happening all over. Our doctors are trying to resist the Gestapo but to no avail. Sorry. You really should be allowed to stay here for another few weeks."

A few days later my usual doctor told me that my condition was good enough for a short stroll to take in fresh air, and perhaps go to a cafe for a strudel. I can't go in my hospital pajamas, where can I find a uniform? "No problem, I'll send someone." Shortly after comes an NCO. He limps a little. He takes my measurements and casts a glance on my patient card.

"Ah! You're an NCO like me! I'll make you a great uniform. It will take a few days." Then he whispers: "You know, when the doctor approves a new uniform it means: return to the front in no time! I know that story. I was among the first in the attack on the Soviet Union. I was born in 1915. Even as a simple soldier, I am aware that the Russians were not prepared for the surprise attack by Hitler. Like for many of us that guy never inspired much confidence. You're not by any chance a Nazi?"

He went on: "I am Catholic and my father was arrested in 1934 as anti-Nazi. I was born in Frankfurt am Main, my father sold his business in 1934 to leave Nazi Germany. I came to Austria with his family, to Graz. Four years later, in 1939 Hitler annexed Austria. I was drafted into the Wehrmacht in a Panzer division. I was seriously injured, for me the war was over. I was appointed to the rank of sergeant and I received the Iron Cross 1st class. After my convalescence in Graz I requested a position in the hospital center of Cortina. For eighteen months, I work here, as a tailor. If you need anything, do not hesitate to ask" he said, laughing.

I thanked him but I was thinking of the wounded fellow who had been in the ambulance with me. I wanted to find that man who had worked in the transport staff and who seemed so well informed.

The next day, I saw the nurse from another hotel chatting with one of our nurses. I listened. She was talking to her about one of the wounded, a funny guy, never short of good jokes. He has these 'wandering hands'. "When we redo his bandages, you cannot not miss it, his sex reacts like clockwork!" The two women were laughing heartily. I thought this is surely my man. I approach them and tell them that I am looking for my friend, I describe him: "Are you talking about him?" It's him! The nurse asked my name. "My name will not tell him anything because we had no time to introduce ourselves. If you could just tell him to come to see me at the hotel and ask for sergeant Aloÿs Pappert."

The next morning she tells me that my friend is waiting for me at the reception. I stay in my pajamas. Indeed, my neighbor from the ambulance is here. He wears the uniform of an NCO, his arm in a sling. "Happy to see you!" before adding in a whisper: "It smells pretty bad here!" I see what he means ... I tell him briefly about the tailor. "We absolutely have to stay in touch. Once your uniform is ready, call me. Here is the number. Ask for sergeant Hans Kieler. It is urgent! I saw a kiosk in the lobby which sells newspapers, soap, toothpaste, toothbrushes, all that stuff. Here is what you'll do: buy two tubes of toothpaste, but only the brand Blendax, not any other, and a toothbrush. It is cheap and it's very important, you see. From now on we must do everything before we are put on the next train to Germany, and that will not be long, believe me." He says good-bye and turns away.

The next afternoon the tailor called me pretending that there were still some steps to take before he can finish my new uniform:

"Listen to this: in a week many wounded will get here, and the doctors are under orders to make room for them. All the guys almost healed will be sent to the front! The others will be repatriated to Germany. Do you want me to finish your uniform tomorrow night or only in two days?"

- As fast as possible.

- All right, pick it up tomorrow afternoon. I will work overtime.

I phone Hans to tell him that we can see each other the next day.

- I will be at your hotel at 2pm. Do not forget to bring your purchases."

When we meet he goes straight to the newsstand without even greeting me. Then, while pretending to read "Der Stürmer", he whispers to me: "In five minutes in front of the hotel." What is this, a treasure hunt? At the hotel, a young woman at the reception asks me if I am Aloÿs. She hands me an envelope that contains a brief message: "I am at Café Astoria. Be careful." With a nonchalant air I go to the Astoria. The Cafe is full of soldiers and civilians. I approach the table that Hans has chosen and ask, as if I did not know him, if there is a free chair. He plays the game, folds his newspaper and invites me to sit down. I order a strudel and a glass of South Tyrol Gewürztraminer.

He asks me if I have the toothpaste tubes. I have them. I slipped one under his journal. It's like being in a spy movie, with toothpaste perhaps hiding some microfilm! He finally decides to explain:

"We both had an attack of malaria and the doctors know that at any moment there can be a relapse. Listen carefully: tonight you go brushing your teeth like always. Place yourself so no one really can see what you are doing, but everyone can hear you brush your teeth. By the way, how many are still in your room?"

"There were four, but two were declared cured, they left the hotel yesterday."

"Good, very good. So after brushing, discreetly swallow half of the tube, you swallow quickly, as quickly as possible. I warn you it's really disgusting, but hold on, do not spit it out. Your survival depends on it. Then you go to bed. After an hour you will begin to shiver and you call the nurse. She will take your temperature and you will be moved to a malaria room. Quinine injections, the usual treatment. It's not safe, but you are young, your heart will manage. Never forget that we are being watched. Do not tell anyone, I repeat: no one! This is the only way to get together on the train to Germany. The war will end soon, we must make sure that we will survive to be among those who will help in the liberation of Germany. Come! Don't look so glum! Good luck, and see you on the train to freedom!"

Hans had cleared up some of the mystery but this man remained enigmatic for me. Has he told me a 'canard' with this story about toothpaste? If this would really work, would I commit a crime by evading being sent back to the front? I hesitated but the fear of being sent back to the front before I had enough strength to deal with it was stronger than my misgivings. Go for this 'malaria' operation!

Bent over my sink, I followed exactly the instructions. Lightning speed of the reaction. It's just then that I remember to call the nurse. I woke up in a special train compartment for patients with malaria. We probably were grouped together to make treatment easier. The train had left Cortina and we were already crossing the border into Germany at Lienz, Austria. I felt weak, tired, but happy! I put miles between the war and myself. I was on the train to freedom! At least I believed so.

The day after our departure my friend Hans surfaces. He asks to be placed in the same compartment with me. My neighbor, a corporal, kindly agrees to give up his seat. We at last get to know each other.

Hans was born in 1920 in Offenbach, a town near Frankfurt am Main, into a family of socialists. A heart condition allowed him to do his military service in administration in Germany. He specialized in communication, telex, etc. In 1943, he was transferred to the headquarters of the 90th Division in Italy, where he was well placed to be informed about everything. He explained why the six fighter bombers flew over our Red Cross ship before turning north and why our boat docked in a port other than the planned: the pilots had seen that our boat actually was carrying wounded and sick. As we were sailing northward there was already another boat in our slip carrying the Red Cross signs but our trucks were loading it with boxes of ammunition and military equipment. The Allied command had learned about this from the Italian resistance. By using the flag of the Red Cross for military purposes, the German army had committed a war crime. The Allied were confused and then made terrible mistakes such as the attack on our ambulance convoy.

Always on the alert, Hans continues with a low voice:

"One day at headquarters, I received a personal message for a superior officer. Immediately after, some NCO rushed into my office and took me to military security. Point blank, he ordered me to show him all messages addressed personally. Just like that! So I replied, slightly ironic, "Even the messages for the general?" You know what he did? He shoved his SS ID under my nose, with his photo and Gestapo stamp. Before leaving, he said: "You have never seen me but rest assured we are everywhere. We know you are a social democrat and we are watching you with particular care. Heil Hitler!" Then he leaves. Believe me, since that meeting I distrust everybody and I am right. Nothing like that at Cortina d'Ampezzo? Well, I spotted two Gestapo spies. Do you understand why I was dealing in so many mysteries? A malaria nurse has kept me safe. She is a very good friend, she agreed to help me. Before I landed in your field hospital, she said we would remain in contact, she would give me messages by a trusted friend. We will meet again someday. At Cortina, a nurse handed me a short message: "Prudence, I kiss you." Well, now you know the rest of my story because we have lived through so much together."

My turn to tell him about my search to find him. Now we laugh with this story. The only thing that obsesses Hans is that the Gestapo has infiltrated everywhere.

Two more days on the train and we are in Aschaffenburg, between Frankfurt and Würzburg. Our hospital looks nothing like a real hospital. Last year, it was still the primary school in the city with four three-story buildings. A nurse gives us the story:

"You see there, it was the main school in town. We moved military hospitals increasingly to small towns, it's safer."

What about the students?

"We sent them to the country in simple barracks built in haste, and they continue their studies but, at the same time, they are obligated to undergo military and political training! At 17, out you go to the front! Those that are more sturdy are shipped to the Waffen-SS. For others it is the Wehrmacht or air defense, cannon fodder nonetheless. The Gestapo, they are everywhere, even here I know one."

- Show him to me."

- OK.

Back to the malaria section on the third floor, among my companions. Hans is already there. "You know where I can make a telephone call, Hans?" He leads me to a corner beside the infirmary.

Along the way, I want to make him aware of the presence of a guy from the Gestapo. "The nurse promised to show me the guy at the first opportunity."

On the phone, I tell Josef where I am, and to tell my parents. There is no question of staying two hours on the phone! I always had the Gestapo in mind, knowing that wiretaps are one of their specialties. Hans phoned his father but the communication was quickly interrupted. This does not surprise me. "Listen, Hans, your father is registered as anti-Nazi and his line is tapped just as mine." The nurse beckons me. "I'll be right back." She wanted to show me the Gestapo man, talking with a soldier. Could he be the only one? How to know with more than 700 wounded and sick crowded in here? The nurse shared some of her confidences:

"Before coming here I was in the military hospital in Wurzburg, for one year. There the Gestapo was to decide who was healed or not. The doctors in the military hospitals in Germany often were of an advanced age and those that were young typically had been seriously wounded. In either case they were unsuitable for use in a hospital at the front but they were always afraid of being arrested by the Gestapo if they do not support the Gestapo's verdicts. You and many others from the third floor, we will declare you cured in good time, and then you will be will sent home for three weeks of sick leave. Then you will receive a letter with your orders and present them to get your rail tickets. After that, welcome back to the front!"

Leaving the nurse, I said to myself, now you have to live under Gestapo control. Imagine that my father had lived with that sword hanging over his head ever since 1933! I never thought that this threat would also fall on me, on soldiers, NCOs and officers of the Wehrmacht!

Lying on my bed, I continued to ponder. Our democratic civilization, our freedom to think, to criticize was devoured by the Nazi dictatorship. There is no room for a hierarchy of values, intellectual, aesthetic or moral. Nothing more than fear and suspicion. Turning my head I see our Gestapo guy sitting on a bed in a corner of the room! He reads and, from time to time, looks up from his book. What can he really think, this little robot dictator who obvious was relishing his new-found power?

The doctor arrives to examine Hans and other malaria section patients. It's time for the temperature check: 99°F for me. Then the doctor goes away. We were told that starting tomorrow evening we will be part of the aerial alarm service. All of a sudden the prospect of being declared healed prematurely becomes a danger for us.

The next morning, after breakfast, we gathered on the building's roof to listen to an older officer. "Alarm stations operate 24 hours, seven days a week. A first shift of six men will start at 8pm, after dinner, until 4am. Eight hours of surveillance duty. Ideally, there will be a warning at least an hour before the bombers get here. We will then start the sirens, seven soundings in a row: 'Full alarm'. The staff will take all the wounded to the shelter. If the danger passes, we will give the 'all clear' signal. It's not very complicated."

At 6pm, everyone is getting ready to go to the canteen except the Gestapo man who does not move from his bed. As we leave, I whisper to Hans: "Did you forget something?" "Oh, wait, I forgot the Army News, it will give me an excuse." He picks up his newspaper, saying loudly: "As always very interesting reading, it makes you feel so much better!" As he leaves the field of view, he whispers to me: "This guy has the best job!"

Two hours later, we're on the roof and take over the equipment, two night binoculars and two guns. Again Hans is the man for the job. He knows how to use everything! Around 11pm, the phone rings: Alarm! Sirens howling, getting combat ready, commotion in all buildings. We watch the sky. In town, the lights went out, also around us, one after the other. Around midnight, a distant roar of explosions, the sky turns red. According to Hans, they are bombing the city of Darmstadt, not too close. "I know their technique. They make a first pass to test our air defense. A few weeks after they will pound it for good."

At 4am, the end of our shift. To bed! Before falling asleep, I think about our situation: permanent fear! Only the revolt of the elite of the army could deliver us from the Nazi dictatorship. On that hope I fall asleep.

At 8am, Hans wakes me up. "Get up! We take a shower and line up for breakfast. Today, it seems we take tea with the locals. This is a ruse by the Nazis, to get soldiers to talk with a family nearby."

Not much later, a charming girl is waiting at the door of the hospital and invited me to ride with her in a fancy Mercedes car. Half an hour away and we are in front of a beautiful villa. Her parents receive me. The father is tall and imposing, the mother is very elegant, thin face, brilliant blue eyes, intelligent, the other daughter just like her. Her name is Liselotte or Lilo. She is 17, her sister 19.

We go to the lounge for tea accompanied by a fruit tart. The conversation does not flow, the situation lacks spontaneity. What shall I say to break the ice? I retrace my brief military career, noting that I am not a volunteer and that in three months I will be 20, God willing! I watched from the corner of the eye the glances of admiration that Lilo threw me. Her father is an entrepreneur and does not hide his pride in his work. Since 1943, he has been short of skilled workers, only those too old for military service. The rest of his team is formed of prisoners of war.

He is mainly busy with clearing the bombed cities and building temporary structures, if the customer can pay. The government, the town administration, they do nothing?

He shrugs. Somehow, the afternoon ends, we must return. I thank the family for their hospitality. Lilo makes her mother renew the invitation for the next day. Okay. Lilo accompanies me to the door and, before leaving, slips me a paper with her address. "Maybe you can give me yours tomorrow?" "Of course, with great pleasure." She blushes.

The next afternoon, as expected, back with Lilo. This time, the atmosphere is more relaxed and we spend a very pleasant afternoon, and I dare ask if I can make a call to my brother in Fulda. The father has no objection. In his office, there is an extension phone.

"Nobody is listening in?"

I was right in asking this question.

"I do not know, but it's possible. There is a second phone not registered at the postal office."

"Isn't this dangerous for the postmaster?"

The father says: "You know, he and I are both members of the Nazi party. For me it was good for my business, for him it was an obligation. Since Stalingrad, we both realized that Hitler would never win the war. The British and Americans are not far from the borders of Germany, and the Soviets win battle after battle."

"Everyone knows that! Why don't you create a kind of resistance with reliable friends? It's never too late."

- No comment.

Then my call comes through:

"Hello Josef, in four days I'll ..." He interrupts me: "Yes, I know. Have a nice trip and see you soon." He hangs up.

No doubt the line is tapped. "Everything fine?" asks Lilo's father.

"No, this direct line is apparently tapped!"

As before, Lilo drove me back to the hospital. I gave her my address and asked her not to write to my parents as it may be very dangerous for them and even to her family. I kissed her, leaving her a vague hope of a reunion after the war, a 'white lie'. "Auf Wiedersehen, Lilo, or rather farewell." So will end many meetings in wartime, under the reign of terror, including in her own family.

*

On July 20, after breakfast, the doctor tells us that the administration is preparing our initial documents for our convalescent leave. Nothing to report, total routine, but then, at the end of lunch, we are informed that, for security reasons, no one could leave the hospital in the afternoon. Bizarre, these instructions. I was going to talk to 'my' nurse.

When she sees me, she makes a discreet sign. Not now. I walk away. She follows me, at a distance. In the corridor, I pass two

Gestapo men flanking an unknown guy that has the appearance of a superior.

Meanwhile 'my' nurse catches up with me. The news is not reassuring. All phones lines were cut. Only the line of the head doctor was still working, but used by the Gestapo. "The radio in the library?" "Cut, too." I returned to our room. The bed of the Gestapo guy is empty. By 10 am the guy shows up and goes on as if nothing had happened. Half an hour later, a speaker made a sensational announcement: "Our Führer Adolf Hitler has succumbed to an attack! We expect more news." Obviously we did not know that the attack had taken place much earlier in the morning!

In our room and everywhere bursts of cries of joy. Hans finally says: "The bastard is dead! The end of the war is coming soon!" I did not hide my satisfaction. Hans points to the Gestapo guy.

In the canteen, a huge hubbub. Lots of laughter from my comrades. "Hans, listen to this, our bad guy from the Gestapo is coming after us. I fear the worst. Those bastards are capable of anything. Watch out!" In the queue to the buffet, 'my' nurse whispers in my ear:

- Don't trust any one! There's danger in the air.
- You think it's a setup?
- Yes, I think that's it.

Dinner drags on, with the sole topic of conversation, Hitler's death. When we finally return to our room, the light is already on, but still no Gestapo. Night has fallen, Hans comes out with three friends. Shortly after he returned, he is followed by the Gestapo guy, his face set in anger.

Twenty minutes later, the speaker again. New announcement: "Our Führer Adolf Hitler was only slightly injured. As always, Providence was with him. He handed the command over our air force, navy and ground forces to the Minister of the Waffen-SS, Heinrich Himmler. Most of the plotters have been shot. Others and their families will be hanged or sentenced to spend the rest of their lives in prison."

A leaden silence hangs over the room. Time for a furtive glance toward the Gestapo guy. Then the room is plunged into darkness. Blackout. When the light comes back, his bed is empty. An atmosphere of conspiracy is all around. We hear a whistle, voices in the yard, and nothing more.

The next morning at 6 am our Gestapo guy, accompanied by another, announces that this morning we will have breakfast in two groups. He began to read the names of the first group, about half of the occupants of our room. I'm part of it. Not Hans. We are given the order to gather our belongings and take them back because we no longer will stay here. Exchange of small signs with Hans, and we go out. In the canteen, I am having lunch with the adjutant next to me. He tells me that I am lucky.

- But why ?

- Because you leave the hospital today for your three week sick leave.

- The others?

No comment.

After lunch, we are paid our salaries, included three weeks of leave, and given all the usual documents. Everything goes very fast. At noon I was ready. In the hall of the railroad station I see the adjutant. He bought two newspapers. He gives me one saying:

"Here's the truth. The Gestapo played a satanic game with us. All communication with the outside are cut, they informed us of the attack five or six hours after it occurred. The goal was to hear everybody's views. You know, I have known for quite some time that the Nazis had infiltrated the army. I'm suspicious of everything. Anyway, where are you going?"

- Fulda and then Hünfeld. And you?

- Limburg. My train leaves in an hour and a half, I think yours is in half an hour. It's time to go.

- Since you know so much, maybe you can tell me what will happen to our other comrades?

- It's simple, they will be interrogated by the Gestapo. Most will be sent to a penal battalion, I don't need to draw a picture

- On the contrary, it may surprise you but so far this term 'penal battalion' was not part of my vocabulary.

- Really? I'm 26, I was wounded twice on the Eastern front and in Italy, like you. The first time I saw a penal battalion was in late 1943. The Waffen-SS sent those guys into the most desperate actions against the Red Army and when almost all had been killed, our own Panzers rolled over the dead and the wounded to take the Russians by surprise. That's what they do with penal battalions.

On these sinister words we parted. Truly, a sad goodbye. This cursed war, certainly lost but not over, not yet!

May God protect us...

*

CHAPTER 7

The Home Front in Disarray

The train home was overcrowded, full of soldiers and civilians. I squeezed into a compartment already occupied by five soldiers, two women and a girl. I immersed myself in the newspaper to learn more about of this bombing strike against Hitler, as far as one could trust the newspaper. Reading about the details of the attack was exciting enough but the news about the repressions of the entire nation that followed were bad indeed. The odious rules of conduct of the Waffen-SS under the command of Himmler had become the new standard of behavior for the entire German armed forces, much to the chagrin of the Wehrmacht. Now all members of the Wehrmacht would have to salute each other with the hated "Heil Hitler!" with arm raised instead of the traditional 'hand on the helmet'. All Wehrmacht units came under the command of generals who were known to blindly obey the Führer. On top all Wehrmacht officers would more than ever be under the surveillance of the Gestapo. I could not help but think back to the diabolical trap that the Gestapo had set for us in our Aschaffenburg military hospital. The Gestapo probably had done the same elsewhere to ferret out anyone critical of their oppression. I felt terrible that my friend Hans who was the very one who had warned me against the Gestapo had fallen into their trap! Such a revolting fate....

The first images of Fulda showed the appalling damage done by the Allied bombing. Straight off the Hünfeld train station I went to my sisters Clara and Catherina. I find Oskar, my brother-in-law in his concrete products factory. It does not take long to come to the main topic of conversation ... Does he think he will be drafted? Him? Never! The cardiologist at the Hünfeld military hospital had declared him unfit for military service. I thought to myself - let's hope the Gestapo will not override his doctor's diagnosis!

- Anyway, the war will be over soon and Nazi Germany will disappear.

"My dear Oskar, I tell you the war is far from over. Now with Himmler in charge the Nazis will not rest until all Germany is destroyed. Many people will still die, but Germany, the new Germany will be revived by people like you. I pray to God to protect me so that I can see that day. Between us, what have I known of our Germany in my youth? Dictatorship, fear and the madness of an Austrian corporal leading our country into misery. Look! Even some in your family have became members of the Nazi Party. Maybe, they changed their minds since, but in the meantime they have not ceased to follow the Nazis' orders!"

Then there were my sister Clara and Caterina. We hugged warmly and both started to reel off their own horrors of the war. Catherina's husband, head of the Fulda train station, miraculously had survived the repeated train station bombing. So many had not been so fortunate. Clara told me how pilgrims from various regions had gathered on the Feast of Pentecost to attend an open-air mass in front of a huge cross, in defiance of the Nazis. Allied planes dropped several bombs on the gathered crowd. Result: more than thirty people dead and hundreds injured... and no doctors! These people had already lived through the war, and had suffered a lot. How can we ever understand such absurd cruelty?

I asked Oscar if he could find a taxi for me to go to my parents. Of all the taxis in service before the war, there remained only two, one of which was driven by our friend Josef Schwab.

Huge embraces at the reunion with my parents! For ages they had no news of me, even though Josef kept them informed as much as he could. My father and mother seem much older, their health undermined by worries. They are well aware that for me the war was not over. My mother phoned Willy Unverzagt. When he had joined us, the conversation begins with the last days of my Italian campaign, my injury, the malaria incident, Cortina d'Ampezzo and then the train to Aschaffenburg. Meanwhile, my mother prepared an 'ersatz' coffee and Hedwig came with a cake.

There is literally no other topic than about the hoped for end of this war. I never tire of reminding everyone that it is not over, this cursed war. Sure, the Americans are coming closer, and so are the Russians, however dark that prospect, but anyway, many soldiers and civilians still will go down. Hitler had promised 'a Thousand-year German Empire' and too many people believed it. Our neighbor, a former Nazi, comes to join in the conversation and goes even further: "You're right, Aloÿs. I had four sons and four daughters. The account is simple: I still have four daughters. Erna, the eldest, was never indoctrinated. The other three have done work in some service and returned with their heads full of Nazism. They accuse me of defeatism. No way to reason with them!" Then he asked my father if by chance he would have a little bit of schnapps, just to cheer up. He drank a lot of it, frankly a bit too much. Sometime later he died of cirrhosis, before seeing the end of the war.

Suddenly fatigue overcomes me, nothing else to do or say other than apologize to my parents: "I'll have to go tomorrow to the Hünfeld military hospital. I'm on leave but still recovering. Good evening everyone…"

The next day, it's again Josef Schwab who comes to drive me to the hospital in his taxi. He is on time. Twenty minutes driving gives us twenty minutes to talk about everything and nothing. Josef Schwab knows my brother. They worked together at the railway. He is an invalid, he has lost half a foot in a train accident. This is why he became a taxi driver. I told him what got me to the hospital, and he leads me directly to the department for tropical diseases.

The doctor is my father's age. I say hello but he takes me quickly into his office. The door closed, he hastens to explain: "You were committing a serious error! Have you forgotten that the military is now to say 'Heil Hitler?' Do not forget either! Here we have many patients, most of them with serious injuries. When they barely can stand we must declare them healed and they go on sick leave for three weeks and then? You can guess. The Gestapo controls everything and dictates what we can and cannot do. I was in the war of 1914 to 1918 as a young doctor in the German colonial army in Cameroon. It is there that I specialized in tropical diseases. There were many sick soldiers and many more civilians suffering from all kinds of tropical diseases, so I gathered a lot of experience. In the beginning of the war we had very good relations with the French who occupied neighboring Togo. There was virtually no border between us. In 1915 a phony war began and a year later we were taken prisoner by the French colonial army. In our hospital we had to focus our attention on the French soldiers. For our own, there was no medicine left. Finally, I was able to leave Cameroon in 1920 on a French boat and I went back to Germany, where I continued to practice my specialty. So what can I do for you?" I showed him my records and asked for medication to avoid a malaria relapse. He prescribed four weeks worth of quinine. I thanked him and left.

I wanted to spend the next day to visit my aunt and her son, my cousin Amand. What can a soldier on leave talk about if not war? This time, Amand asked me to be considerate and to talk about everything else, and for good reason. Amand told me that my poor aunt could not overcome the death of her two sons at the Russian front.

You know, added Amand, imagine that here, of 72 villagers, we had 18 people dead on the Russian front, and six men returned seriously injured! In addition, two of the six remaining farmers were arrested last week, supposedly because they sold their produce on the black market! Pure invention! I asked the mayor and the deputy prefect to intervene to free them because they are completely innocent. The harvest this year was not very good, and I have not enough help. One wonders how long all this will last?

"You think I could come to help you with the potato harvest? I could perhaps get some time off from my battalion."

The next visit was for my brother in the Fulda barracks. He told me to wait for him in a nearby restaurant. Ten minutes later he arrived on foot.

- Well, my dear Joseph, times have changed! The last time you had a car at your disposal!

- Yes, before I had a boss with whom I got along very well. At 45, he was considered too old to fight. But six months ago he was still sent to the Eastern Front ... In its place came a veteran from the 14-18 war, 55, flanked by an SS captain who supervises us all, gives orders, controls all communications and opens the mail. Do not forget the Hitler salute, especially outside.

We had lunch of a bratwurst accompanied by potato salad and a beer. For the third time, I told the story of my life as a soldier ... We remained pensive. Josef then asked me if I knew my future assignment.

- Probably Zwickau in Saxony, because our infantry division is based in Zwickau. I expect my orders about September 10-12.

- Ask Hedwig to let me know and I'll come to see you off. You know the worst is before you?

Yes, I had no illusions about it, the worst was waiting for me. We went out. The street was full of soldiers. Always that damned 'Heil Hitler' salute to my brother. Heil Hitler! here, Heil Hitler! there, Heil Hitler! everywhere. We had a hard time saying good bye. Josef, before crossing the gates of the barracks threw me a little smile and a wave of the fraternal hand.

On the way to the station, I was trying to gather my thoughts. What had happened to my youth? Thrown away for what? Perhaps lost forever. Hatred and anger came over me, hatred for Hitler and his gang, anger against all those who had helped him get into power, including the old senile President Hindenburg. On the train I remembered a conversation with my father. I was about 12, I came home from school, edgy, angry. My father said: "My son, anger only express weakness. To become strong, we must remain master of our thoughts and our actions. It is the same with fear, it can become paralyzing. Try to take control of these issues." When I was 10 and 12, I was shy, and it did not escape my father that I was afraid also. On the night of May 11 to 12, 1944, in Italy I had proven that I had been completely cured of all that.

Back at home my father asked me to take a walk with him. So far I had kept my encounter with God at Monte Cassino to myself but now I felt strong enough to share it with him. "Do not worry about me, father, I do not know my future in any detail, but I am sure to return home one day. God is with me. The war will end, perhaps in six or eight months. Soon I may be able to tell you where it will end for me, most certainly on the Eastern Front. I may be captured by the Red Army, but then this will be the end of the war. There will be a long time without news from me. Trust me, I will return."

"Yes, Aloys, I believe we will meet again. You're different from Josef. You deeply believe in God, and he will help you to come back."

Sunday was nice and quiet, a fine family day. In the morning, at mass, most women wore black, sadness written on their faces. I noted the absence of the tailor's wife and his daughters. My father told me that the tailor had died in the East, and his wife had left the area with her daughters.

According to Josef, the captain wanted to see me, and it was perhaps to tell me about a promotion or a decoration or to warn me against the SS: "I heard this morning on the radio that the city of Darmstadt was wiped off the map in the night of September 11 to 12. Of the 100,000 inhabitants, nearly 13,000 are dead and 70,000 are homeless, not counting the wounded and those burned by phosphorus bombs. We understand now that the bombing of civilians in cities without air defense and with no military presence are a part of the Allied's program to break the morale of the Germans, an idea promoted by Travers Harris, the commander of the Royal Air Force. It seems that the goal is to push our population to revolt against the Nazis. They did not understand that since 1933 Germany was under the total domination of the Nazis, and after the attempt on Hitler's life the SS and the Gestapo turned the country into a ghetto!"

Long and heavy silence.

" Father, you did your apprenticeship in Darmstadt, right?"

"Yes, in Darmstadt, with the best master saddler and upholsterer, from 1902 to 1905, and in 1906 I got my diploma. I had a chance to join my uncle who at the time was chamberlain of the Grand Duke Ernst Ludwig of Hesse. He lived in the magnificent castle of Darmstadt. My uncle had a fine military career and had learned several languages, he spoke perfect French and English. At the end of the 1914 war he went to the United States with his wife and three of his sons. In early 1920, I received a letter from my uncle who asked us to join him in America. I could not leave my country, cut myself off from my roots. I still remained in contact with him for several years until his death in 1925."

On September 13 my cousin Amand and I go to the mayor who is married to my godmother. He is willing to support my request to work for a few weeks on Amand's farm for helping in harvesting potatoes. He said he will send my request to my reserve battalion for approval. He promises to hand over my file in person to the sub-prefect and it will be at my reserve battalion in five or six days. I thanked him and we had a great lunch with my godmother. "The sub-prefect is a Nazi but mostly we get everything we want from him. I am on good terms with him, every fortnight he passes by our farm and leaves with a sausage or a ham ..."

The next three days passed quickly. On the 17th I was on the train to Zwickau to report to my battalion. My mother wanted to prepare a package with food for me but I refused: would I not be back in a few days to pick potatoes?

My trip to Zwickau was a long one. Nothing worked as planned. The Erfurt train station had been bombed and we had to continue our trip by bus. We arrived at my destination very late. I ran to the battalion office to apologize.

No problem! Everybody and everything was delayed in these days.

*

Chapter 8

Discovering the Power of My Faith

"Sergeant Pappert reporting to duty", with the somewhat uncomfortable exchange of the odious "Heil Hitler!".

From behind his desk, the senior officer scrutinizes me:

"So you are Pappert! I read your file. In Italy, you have demonstrated a great sense of responsibility and a lot of courage. Your company commander, Captain Vetter, wrote a highly favorable report. I am pleased to inform you of the result of his accolades: I will make you my adjutant. In addition, I have the honor to present the Iron Cross 1st class to you. I already asked the tailor to come to make the necessary changes to your uniform. It's a matter of a few minutes. As we wait for him to do his job we can spend some time to get to know each other."

The tailor leaves, and the Major continues:

"First I have to tell you that the 94th Division no longer exists. Too many losses in the battle of Monte Cassino. The remnants of the division were merged with another infantry division. As a result, we have become a training battalion for recruits."

His name was von Kagenau and he had been in the 14-18 war. Like everyone else, he had gone into that war with great enthusiasm, knowing he would be back home in a few months. Just like the French he got trapped in the horrible trench warfare. Promoted to major and battalion commander, he had lost half of his men at Verdun and he was seriously wounded and lost a foot. He was then made a major in the reserve. Today, at 58, he had to return to serve in the Zwickau regiment.

"Let me tell you that I saw big changes in Germany. It's sad." He went on with the tale of his experiences ...

"A final word: during the last two months we have an officer of the Waffen-SS here, with the rank of captain. Before him, there was a Gestapo guy disguised as simple soldier, who was reporting everything to his superiors. This new one is a 26 year old, bristling with decorations. A very dangerous guy. You will not see him right away because you will leave this evening for your two week potato harvest holiday with your cousin Amand Wassermann. When you return, you will begin your work under my command."

The tailor came back, my new uniform under his arm. The major took me to a small conference room where some NCOs were assembled. The major briefly introduced me as his new warrant officer and then fixed the Iron Cross 1st Class on my uniform. Applause. "Our new adjutant Aloÿs Pappert is not quite 20, but has a lot of military experience which will be very useful in the training of recruits."

Together we all raised a glass of beer, and the major left. The warrant officers and NCOs flooded me with many issues. One of them took me aside to tell me: "Be careful when you return. We are all monitored by this SS guy, including the major. This SS captain is much decorated and has a very strong influence on young recruits." I cut him short saying that I knew this issue, we would be talking about it again later.

The administration had done its job. All the documents for my leave were prepared perfectly. A last "Heil Hitler!" and at 8pm I was on the train to Hünfeld, arriving there in the morning.

What a surprise! My mother holds me in her arms, ecstatic in amazement. She immediately called my father, amazed to see me so soon again. Neither had believed that my attempt to get time off to help my cousin Amand with his harvest would happen.

- You got the adjutant's stripes! noticed my father.

- Yes, there was a small ceremony in my honor in the presence of the battalion's NCOs. But I've got to thank my sponsor and Amand.

Amand immediately led me to the mayor, a very nice guy: "My word, here you are as adjutant with the Iron Cross 1st class!" It was almost as Amand fell from the clouds, he had not noticed! The mayor invited us to lunch. As always, I was expected to tell my war stories and my impressions of Zwickau. "It was probably a very beautiful city but it has suffered several bombings aimed at the Horch and Audi car factories that now manufacture trucks and light armored vehicles for the army. As you can imagine the surrounding parts of the city suffered terribly. Our barracks were not affected as they are quite far from the factories." Then I told them of the warnings they had given me about the SS captain.

- It's the same here, adds Amand, the Gestapo controls everything, even our sub-prefect in his brown-Nazi gold uniform. We call these guys 'golden pheasants.' Fortunately we have good relations with the one here, otherwise you would not have had your leave. And your next destination?

- Surely the Eastern Front.

This feels like a cold shower, as if announcing someone's death.

Amand laughed when I asked him for instructions when we began picking potatoes. I said goodbye to my godmother and joined my parents for a pleasant and joyful evening at home.

After refilling my quinine prescription in the military hospital of Hünfeld, I visited our priest to take a look at the register of my friends and acquaintances who had died 'for the Fuehrer'. Going through these sinister records, I came across the Trott name. The eldest son, a fighter pilot, was shot down over the English Channel during the Battle of Britain; the second, Otto, died in

129

Russia, the third, Richard, seriously injured early 1944 in the East. At least he will come home again.

Finally, the last brother, Bernard. I had known him well, he was one of my best friends. Drafted early in 1944, the register tells me he died suddenly in August on the Eastern front. A terrible shock. I was unable to hold back tears.

- Maybe you could go over to the Trotts, suggested the priest, it will be good for them. I hope I shall not see you in my registry! God willing, you will return safely, and he gives me the sign of the cross.

- I promised my parents that I will return, because God is with me.

- I see that you have an unwavering faith.

- I will come on Saturday to confess and we'll see each other at Sunday Mass.

Trott's father was a cabinet maker, and I had known him as a very strong man, always cheerful. In what state would I find him now? His wife welcomes me. My appearance triggers a flood of tears as she holds me in her arms, thanking me, and between sobs: "Your friend Bernard ... hardly 18 ... Dead! And for what?" I could hardly hold on to myself, hearing these cries of a wounded mother. At this point Richard enters, on crutches, "Ah! Aloÿs, glad to see you! As you can see, I'm not in my best form but in a few months I may be walking normally. For me the war is over, and for you?" The father arrives, now like an old man, irretrievably broken. I did not dare ask for news of their two daughters. I knew from my mother that they had been recruited as nurses in military hospitals. What to say to these unhappy people? I was speechless. I do not regret being here because in these times when every word could sound false, only the actual presence of a friend can help.

On the way back I met several acquaintances who greeted me mechanically, without the slightest sign of warmth. Sometimes they bother to ask me when I was going to leave again. Whatever I answer, I felt that people were listening to me but without real interest - they had so many problems of their own. Nobody seemed to have much hope left.

Whenever possible, I avoided the painful issues of the war with my parents. I tried to focus on the joy of being together. Nothing doing, my father could not get out of his sadness.

"Yes, the war is not over, and eventually it will come here, too. Hopefully, you will not be taken by the Red Army but by the Americans. I got to know them. They are heavily armed, very cautious, they do not want to lose their men, certainly not just before the end of the war. When they arrive, if German troops are still in the area, it is essential to convince them to abandon their positions because if they shoot at the Americans their army will not take any risks, they will shell everything into dust. Then, when I return, I will find no one alive! Here there are still men of goodwill. Let them tell the last remaining German soldiers to leave, and ask everyone in town to hang white flags in their windows. Willy Unverzagt and the mayor, you will take a big white flag and go to the Americans. I suggest that you organize a small meeting of friends and I will talk to them after my return from Fulda."

My train trips between Hünfeld and Fulda gave me the opportunity to meditate on all that. I have always used every opportunity to see my parents, and I always invariably faced the same distress, especially of the women and mothers. For it is the mothers who are hurt the most, and they need our letters to comfort them. Whether from Russia, France, or Italy, I wrote regularly and my mother answered immediately. I also wrote to most of my classmates. Sometimes their simple but magnificent poems inspired mothers and their sons, placing them near their hearts during their lives and until their death. I felt a bit guilty admitting to myself that during these times of leave I was closer to my father even though it was my mother who maintained close contact with me. This was not right, I thought. I had to change my attitude. Now, I will express love for my mother as the center of my priorities, reserving contact my father as between men.

Whenever I would look up and watched people in the compartment I had the feeling that I might have expressed my thoughts aloud. Once an elderly woman told me:

- You are still very young, perhaps you're on leave? Do you still have your parents?

- Yes, and I go to Fulda see my brother who was seriously injured in 1943. And you?

- I travel with my daughter and my grandchildren. My daughter lost her husband early in 1943 in Stalingrad. I had two sons, they died in Russia. There are always more tears to shed.

There was hardly anyone to meet without having to face some great misfortune. What could I say except try to comfort them. It was impossible for me not to do so. We all had to stick together with simple words, humble human gestures, such as a small smile for them as I left them in Fulda. They continued their journey into nowhere.

Josef was waiting for me in his office: "This is great! You are not even 20 years old and already you are adjutant with the Iron Cross 1st class! Come, I'll introduce you to my battalion commander." He had been notified of my visit and received me warmly, with admiration for my promotion. Here too, the SS men controlled everything. According to the commander, their SS captain had made sure that the young recruits in training would go to the West and that soon the Americans would cross the Rhine and take them. Then Germany would be invaded and the war on the West would end. Then it was my turn to tell about my impressions of the Zwickau reserve battalion, and my boss, also a veteran of 14-18, and not Nazi. Of course, I had to mention the ever present SS in the Wehrmacht. Our SS captain, unfortunately, was said to be a lot less flexible than their own, a real fanatic.

You could not take two steps without the Hitler salute repeated to the point of absurdity. This theatrical gesture imposed on the military became grotesque. At the restaurant, Josef guides us to a table safe from malicious ears. I just had to get it off my chest that this Hitler salute really starting to get on my nerves. "We are not

SS! We are the Wehrmacht. I have not been appointed adjutant and I was not given the Iron Cross as an SS man but as a sergeant of the Wehrmacht! Of this, I am proud!" Immediately, the commander and Josef advise caution, especially in Germany: "When you are on the Russian front, it will be different." For the moment, as their guest, I will do as they say, but it does not change my opinion. Later, on the street, we say good-bye with the Nazi 'Heil Hitler'.....

*

Back in Hünfeld, my sisters Caterina and Clara had not noticed my decoration. This does not surprise me. The military world was totally foreign to them and I could not blame them. Oskar joined us and we drank the usual 'ersatz' coffee, and ate a semblance of a cake, that was all they could make. I had to leave but not before the customary exchange of good wishes between family: we will see each other again soon, you should not worry about me, I know the dangers of war. One last hug and my Schwab taxi takes me to my parents.

At home I am determined to put into action my recent resolutions: I rush to my mother to embrace her warmly to clearly show her all my love. "Thank you mom, always think of me, pray for me, and I love you. Believe me, I will return, your prayers and my faith in God will help me and protect me." My father asks me if I would want to meet with the mayor: "Since becoming mayor in 1936 and a Nazi party member, I had no further contact with him. I was weary of him. It may be useful to renew our acquaintance."

The next day, the mayor receives me. Significant changes in his office: exit the portrait of Hitler and the Nazi insignia!

"Aloysius, you know better than anyone that the war is lost. My son was at Stalingrad, his last letter dates back to the middle of December 43, then nothing. My daughter is only 25, helping me on our little farm. We have a prisoner of war, a Frenchman, who works with her, they take care of our land. He is a nice man and my daughter fell in love with him and she has two children by him. People do not talk about it, but everyone knows. If someone would complain she will be arrested, and our prisoner executed. I tell you now, so that you don't have to learn about it from others."

"You believed in Hitler, in all his promises, but it is time now to think about what will come later, when he and his clique have disappeared. In six months, the Americans will be at our door steps. We need brave men to do everything to avoid further bloodshed. If you agree, I suggest you arrange a meeting between you, my father, Unverzagt and others."

I saw my father cringe at my recklessness, telling our Nazi mayor to plan something that he knew could cost him his life. To our great astonishment he said: "When do you want to do it? I'm ready."

Wow. What a turn-around!

Only three days more of my home leave! My cousin again led me to the mayor where we came face to face with our infamous local Nazi party chief. He was in street clothes but wore his Nazi insignia. He congratulated me on my promotion and my decoration and added:

- You are only 19 years and just like our Führer, you have the Iron Cross 1st class.

Should I reply or keep my mouth shut?

I decided to let him have it: "Adolf Hitler made the trip from his native Austria to Munich in 1914 to enlist in Germany's Imperial army. During the war he served as a courier, very often facing a deluge of fire. His best friends were Jewish and they formed a friendship saying, "One for all, all for one". Wounded several times, he was appointed corporal in 1916 and received the Iron Cross 2nd class. In 1918, still a corporal, he took two French prisoners, and it was only then that he received the Iron Cross First Class."

Our Nazi chief is amazed, and looking at me:

- How do you know all this?

134

"During the battle of Monte Cassino, I had a former Magdeburg bank manager under my command, a confirmed Nazi. I respect his opinion even though I did not share his views. He was a history buff and knew the life of Adolf Hitler from A to Z. When the Allied launched their offensive, we were almost buried alive under the bombs. I prayed with all my soul. He begged me to pray for him, too. I included him in my prayers but I could not help to ask: So where are the secret weapons of the Führer? In response, he burst into tears! Then we were taken prisoner by the Americans. As he spoke English well, he did not tried to escape while I took to the field as soon as I could, and I re-joined my unit."

The sub-prefect shook my hand and told me I was very brave. "Thanks for the compliment but today true courage is to recognize that the war is lost, although for me and other fighters it is not over. I will perhaps be one of the millions of dead, but I will do as much as I can to help my comrades to survive and return to our country."

Throughout all this, Amand was petrified. On the way back, I reassured him: "You know, Amand, the truth never hurts, it's the opposite, it heals. You'll see your party chief will change his attitude."

At home I did not say anything about this interview. No need to spoil the final moments together. Better use this time to be quiet, happy, and laying as low as possible. Last time to call 'my' Schwab taxi. At night I was on the train to Zwickau.

*

The trip went smoothly. We only stopped once. Lights off, we heard bombers flying over us. They would bomb Leipzig, as we would learn the next day. In the Zwickau station, a car was waiting for me. The driver had just deposited our SS captain heading for Leipzig. We set out towards what would become my 'home'. A sergeant greeted me and offered to take me to my room, informing me in passing that Major von Kagenau had invited me to lunch.

My room was very pleasant, featuring a view of the garden, with a comfortable bathroom. I took a shower, put my things away and went out to tour the buildings. We ate our meals at the mess. Only the commander enjoyed the privilege to have his meals in his apartment. The soldiers were housed in other buildings, in groups of ten, under the command of a corporal.

Around noon, the commander's butler came for me to take me to Major von Kagenau's apartment. I greet him with a 'Heil Hitler!' With a slightly wry smile he starts a conversation about Anton the butler who lost his entire family in the first bombing of Essen. He is now alone in the world and does his military service in Zwickau. "I trust him", Kagenau says. We sit in the living room, Anton serves us schnapps and beer, then disappears.

Without transition, the Major wants to know about my 'harvest holiday'. I review the happenings during these two weeks and add that the general atmosphere is so full of anguish and sadness that I felt that I would be better off in the family of the army just wishing for an end of this war. One question kept running through my mind: why had the SS captain left the barracks in such a hurry?

My commander tells me that after the bombing of Leipzig, the SS man tried to reach his relatives. No news, so he ended up going there. He promised to call. "You have not had the opportunity to meet him. Good for you! He is so full of himself! He is in Leipzig now where his family lives in the big house of his relatives, including his wife and a one year old son. For now, that is all I know. I am waiting for news from him."

The meal took its course until the 'ersatz' coffee. We let go of our thoughts freely, in a relaxed conversation. I asked for news of the French government of Marshal Petain. I still had my military service in Clermont-Ferrand very much in mind in this weird time. I did not know how things had developed in France. The major replied without hesitation:

"France was liberated last August, and Marshal Petain had to flee in a hurry with his entire government. According to the official version he was taken to the Sigmaringen Castle by an SS escort. The truth is that he is the prisoner of the SS. When the Allies arrive in Germany, he will be delivered to the new French government. Despite his age, he faces the death sentence. Just between us, in Germany, the Nazi leaders are beginning to pack up! Even more reason to be weary. They have nothing to lose and may become very vicious."

I'm certainly not going to say the opposite. I had many opportunities to see the Nazi's mindset up close, like the 'golden pheasants' of our Party Chief's ilk. I was not alone in my contempt for them - whenever I would use the term 'golden pheasant' it sparked hilarity.

After the meal, I took leave of my host, warmly thanking him for his confidence:

It seemed that I had impressed the Major with my honesty and my open assertion of my Catholic faith. It is as if I had found in him a new friend, almost a father. We should never disappoint each other.

Back in my quarters, I saw the sergeant with whom I spoke on the first day:

- I know an employee from the office of the SS captain. It seems that he will not return for another week.

- That's all?

- Yes, he did not even know he was in Leipzig.

- Leipzig was bombed. He may have wanted to see the damage more closely. But tell me, what is your name?

- Lothar.

- My name, you know already. And when does our recruit training start?

- Tomorrow morning. I put a questionnaire in your room about your thoughts for the recruit training program. You must complete it and return it to the Major before tonight.

- Have you already filled out yours?

- No. I expected to see you so we can do it together, just to compare ideas.

- You did well. I saw that we have the latest weapons here, machine gun MG 42 and assault rifle StG 44. I know neither one nor the other. Do you?

- I know all about the MG 42 but not the assault rifle. Lothar, go get your questionnaire and join me in my room. We will fill it out together.

That evening, we delivered our questionnaires to the office of commander.

I knew all about the machine gun MG 42 - I had used it myself! It is a terrible weapon, nothing like it. The Allied nicknamed it "Hitler's Texas Chainsaw." It was an insatiable devourer of ammo! I knew less about the new assault rifle StG 44 except that it had impressive fire power. You could equip it with a sniper viewfinder. The StG 44 was of a much higher quality than its Russian Kalashnikov competitor.

By late afternoon, I visited the Major after a message from him asking me to see him before dinner. He greeted me with a broad smile, hands me back my questionnaire, telling me to present my training program for young recruits to all officers and NCOs.

- Major, I am honored by your request, but we have among us officers and NCOs older and more experienced than I.

- That's true, but no one presented a program like yours. And you are the youngest. I think it will be a good thing for all of us. Tomorrow you will have the opportunity to earn the trust and the respect of all those responsible for our training battalion.

I was faced with a new challenge. It's 'make or break'!

At the meeting, the Major first thanked everyone for their suggestions and responses to his questionnaire and then he went on:

"I want to thank especially our young sergeant, the youngest of us, decorated with the Iron Cross First Class. His answers are most useful and completely adapted to our task to give our recruits the best preparation for their coming fight. I would like him to present his ideas himself. If you agree, raise your hand."

Everyone agrees. A last look at the major, the decision is made and I start:

"Major, and my dear comrades. We all know that the war is lost, but it is not over. The Red Army has attacked East Prussia. Our army is defending our territory at great sacrifice, mainly to allow time for civilians to leave the country by sea. Many of the ships will be sunk, but blessed are those who can reach Sweden. On the Western front, the city of Aachen has already fallen. The road is open to the Ruhr. Our battalion is entrusted with the training of new fighters. Major, my dear comrades, we will take this great responsibility very seriously. We will show our recruits to fight well but also how to save their own lives. Do we have any other opinions?"

Silence. I am encouraged. It's fine but I know that everything that will come out of my mouth may be fatal for me when our SS Captain will return. Never mind:

"Dear comrades, I was born Catholic and I will stay so until I die. It is my unwavering faith in God that saved my life and gave me the strength to save the men under my command. Among the young recruits who are here, there are young fanatics. They firmly believe in the ultimate victory through some secret weapons. Politics are not part of my military training. I believe that our young people know nothing about the reality of war other than the sound of 'Heil Hitler!' We will train them hard, and for their own good break their arrogance by our own example of endurance. First we will do the endurance exercises, forced march day and night, carrying the weapons and ammunition boxes filled with stones. We only have two weeks to make them physically fit for the battle field. Remember that singing while marching will help expand their lungs and will clear their minds. After that, we will begin the actual weapons training. No need to draw a picture. One last thing: Major, I'd like to talk to the SS Captain after his return."

I see that many are aghast at my audacity (folly?) to expose myself to this feared SS man. I guess I just wanted to know what goes on in the mind of an SS guy! The Major accepts my last request. An officer takes the floor and, with a smirk, asks what to do next, since he is not Catholic. Returning his smile, I recommend him to check his conscience. The meeting is over, there is much applause in a climate of mutual trust.

The first week of training of our young recruits was intensive and very hard for them. Most were dead tired after nights of training. We did not relent and did not give in to the usual laggards. Everyone getting up at 6 am for the first exercise in the yard. At 7am, breakfast, increasingly meager. At 8am start of the next march, the soldiers loaded down with their weapons and all their gear. We march at a speed of 6 miles per hour, singing to expand our lungs. Then fall to the ground, we continue playing attack, shoot, camouflage, move on elbows, keep down under 'enemy' fire.

I take ten sergeants and corporals of my section and show them my 'zigzag' technique that had been so effective for me when I was under enemy fire. I show them by my own example, not sparing myself from utter exhaustion. The young men look at me with a new respect. This is my first victory over their political indoctrination, showing them that leading is not a matter of party slogans. Training resumes, always intensive.

Back in the barracks, Anton, the butler, came to take me to von Kagenau. The Major wants me to give the officers and NCOs a 'blackboard' description of my basic attack technique. The same evening, at the dinner table, I explain why this is so much needed because the Red Army has so many excellent sharp shooters.

On Saturday, a little free time. I went to the station to call Clara. Lothar was with me and we went for a walk to a dance cafe. The atmosphere was gloomy. Yes, there were many war widows looking for fun and consolation but the time of "fried potato relationships" was over......

On Sunday morning my staff informed me that the SS captain is back and that at the major's request he had invited me to lunch at half past twelve. I was not too sure of myself anymore, and I regretted even having asked for this meeting. I remember the silence that had followed my request. Everyone must have thought I was losing my mind, wanting to throw myself into the lion's den! Never mind.

At half past twelve on the dot, the captain welcomes me into his office.

- Well, Pappert, you have quite a reputation for bravery already!

He serves a schnapps and a beer. We sit in two old armchairs and he tells me that once he had learned of the bombing of Leipzig, he had unsuccessfully tried to reach his own family and decided to go there to see what had happened to them. His first observation: the massive bombardment had not been aimed at the arms factories and the rail station but against civilians. The police had already cordoned off the bombed areas. He had sought to learn more. He was told that the fires were still not under control and he could not get any closer until perhaps the next day. Showing his credentials as SS Captain he then asked the police chief to contact the office of the local Party Chief. Two days more of waiting before he could enter the area. The bombers had not been content with dropping very powerful bombs, they also had added phosphorus bombs that triggered terrible fires. When at last he could reach his parents' home, there was nothing left but a black hole, emitting a burning smell. He tried to find something, a memory, but nothing, absolutely nothing. He could not hold back his tears. Now he showed me a photograph of his parents, his wife and baby. So, even a powerful SS-man had his emotions when it came to the unfortunate fate of his own family! Then he led me into another room for lunch.

The table was set. A young SS man served. The meal was simple, washed down with a glass of beer. I could only express my sincere condolences, adding:

"Captain, the war is not over. Many civilians still are going to die. We in the military, we will end up with a bullet in the head, or shredded by shrapnel, or worse, as prisoners of the Bolsheviks! God save us!"

- You believe in God?

- Yes, I do believe in God. To me, this is a great source of strength. Being in charge of soldiers I will do everything to help them become good fighters but also to know how to save their lives, thanks in part to the powerful weapons we have today.

- Interesting. You know, of course, that we have different beliefs. But I respect a man with convictions. By the way, I received a letter from a friend who was director of Radio Luxembourg until the Americans got there a few months ago. He had to leave this beautiful country to return with his family to Germany. He has a beautiful property in Plauen and he invited me and my wife to come to his home to celebrate the birthday of his daughter. I am obviously not in the frame of mind to go there, but I can offer you to go in my stead this coming weekend. You will meet some lovely people. If you accept, I will inform the Major tomorrow.

- Well, thank you very much, Captain!

- Their birthday celebration will take place next weekend. Make sure that our conversation remains confidential.

Lunch was finished. I got up and I left with the Hitler salute. I returned to my room and stretched out on my bed. As if an invisible inspiration guided my thoughts, I felt that I was right to talk about my faith in God at the account of the terrible misfortune that this SS man had suffered. Who knows, maybe it was a turning point in that man's life. I fell asleep thinking of my poor soldier Ekkard.

*

Next day at lunch the Major reviews my meeting with the SS Captain. Kagenau said I had made a good impression as an instructor. Then the invitation to Plauen comes up. The Major is ready to give me the necessary days of leave until Sunday. The Major asks the tailor to find me a dress uniform. The tailor unearthed an impeccable uniform from his 'reserves'. Some adjustments later, I had changed into a fine representative of our battalion. I was pleased to be able to attend this event.

The last days of instruction pass quickly. Taking leave from the Major, he warns me again: there are too many fanatics out there.

At Plauen, a driver was waiting for me in the lobby of the station with a sign with my name. We left in a very big fancy car. Everywhere, houses in ruins, but some already partially reconstructed by a population that did not give up wanting to lead a 'normal' life. The driver was talkative, he told me that Plauen had already suffered two bombings but the textile mills working for the army were able to resume production.

- The villa of my boss is out of town, in a residential area, naturally."

This man seemed to have a loose tongue, so I questioned him:

- How old are you?

- 59 years and I am the driver for Major Weber since 1937.

- So you are with the SS?

- No, but I knew Dr. Weber's father, I was his driver since 1929. He bought this Horch that year. What a car! When Dr. Weber was appointed director of Radio Luxembourg in 1940, his father recommended me to him and I entered his service.

- Dr. Weber is a doctor?

- No, he is a lawyer. He worked at the Ministry of Propaganda as assistant director of Radio "Gross-Deutschland".

- Are you're married?

- I was married. We lived in Plauen, we had two sons. The first died in Poland, the other in Russia in 1942. My wife did not survive her grief. She died two years ago.

The area we entered was indeed very fine, lined with wealthy residences, but the property of Dr. Weber stood out. At the entrance, a man of medium height greets me. This is the Doctor himself. I shake hands with the usual salutation.

- Nice to meet you. Thorsten sang me your praises. You are almost the same age as my daughter. Welcome. Come, I'll show you around, get a glass of French champagne before the guests arrive.

I meet Dr. Weber' wife and daughter, one as beautiful as the other, brown skin with blue eyes. I gave the perfect kiss on the hand and we head to a lounge where we were served a glass of champagne.

- That Captain of your battalion! Thorsten is full of praise about you.

- Excuse me, I did not know his first name. Yes, he is a good man, he suffered much from the death of his wife and son. He showed me pictures of his family.

- Yes, he told me that you had lunch together, that you are a believer and that I can have complete confidence in you. Tonight we will have a lot of people, including the Party Chief of our state. As far as I know he will come in uniform, all the others will be in civilian clothes. (Another 'golden pheasant', I thought.) I advise you to stay on guard, my daughter will be your chaperone, yes, Marianne?

- With pleasure, answered the girl.

- Come, she will show you to your room. If you want to take a bath, or get some rest, please. Just be here at 7pm for cocktails.

Marianne showed me to my room stating that hers is next to mine. How not to respond with a broad smile? I feel so well that I grew bolder: "I count on you to wake me in time for the party."

The bathroom was remarkable. What luxury! A hot bath! As I ran the bath water, a knock. "Come in! The door is open!" It's Marianne, in a bathrobe, telling me she wants to take a bath with me! What a start of my stay!

These delicious times pass, we lie down on the bed, day dreaming, almost forgetting the time. At 7pm sharp we are in the cocktail lounge. So many people! Marianne's father invites us to join him in a toast to his daughter's birthday. There is a lot of hand-kissing, best wishes, congratulations, compliments, all without a care of the world. I was watching everything and even though I had not seen the opera I thought of Wagner's 'Götterdämmerung'. It was just like watching a strange type of comedy.

The reception was in full swing. Gradually the guests are filing into the dining room. Everyone sat. Marianne is at my side. Marianne's mother is facing the Party Chief, and her father in front of his wife. Conversations are underway, presided over by the Chief, the true image of a fat pig. The meal is served in perfect manner, a well planned menu, Moselle white wines, excellent French red wines.

The Party Chief waited for the servers to leave before talking about his new mission, entrusted to him by Heinrich Himmler. He is commissioned with a program to recruit the very young and the very old to form a new army: the 'Home Guard', a people's militia to assist the Wehrmacht. Well, well! I will get the details later from my major. Of the thirty or forty guests there are only two who wear a uniform: the Party Chief and I.

After dinner the men retire to the library to smoke and drink cognac, women in the tea room. Marianne whispered in my ear: "I have a bottle of champagne chilling, we will slip away quietly." With a knowing smile, her mother approves. Marianne leads me to her room, all in girlish pink and light colors. She closes the door behind us and starts to undress. This is Marianne, a girl who lives for the moment, always ready to love. From the bed to the bathroom, back and forth, always more sensual! Then, after a first glass of champagne, she tells me of the good times in Luxembourg where she had met a young man, a year before his departure. Her father knew nothing of it and her mother gave her good advice. She kept the address of that boy who, according to her, was very enamored with her.

Okay, but my mind was much more on petting than on her reminiscing. It does not take long for Marianne to rush at me like a tiger. The night passed in a flash and in the morning, still in the middle of a dream, a knock on the door: "Marianne, it is time to go down for coffee. Wake up your friend."

We were only four at breakfast in the villa of Dr. Weber.

- Too bad you have not talked to more of my guests, said the Doctor.

- It was worth it, believe me!

- Why is that?

Dr. Weber went on: "After draining a few of bottles of cognac, prudence and the usual mistrust between Party members had gradually evaporated. Gone was the propaganda! We only talked about the end of the war, the coming division of Germany into four zones, about the advance of the Red Army into Saxony. I'll spare you the details but, just between us, I was ashamed of my career in the SS. My father was right, but I did not listen. We believed in the coming of the good times for Germany. I was part of the youth that took power. We were intoxicated by our enthusiasm without seeing too many important members of the party were uneducated and crude, just like our Party Chief. You know, he and his ilk will not leave the country, they will sell themselves out to the new masters. Those Nazis, they will somehow manage to move quietly into communism, become new 'Commissars of the People', these bastards."

- I hope you have already prepared your future in Bavaria in the future American occupation zone. Bavaria is only 50 kilometers away and the population is Catholic.

- You are still young but your judgment is sound! You have convinced yourself for some time already that the war is lost. Doesn't this scare you?

"No, in the contrary. My faith gives me strength to see the future in a different light. This war will still kill thousands of people. As a soldier, I have a moral responsibility vis-à-vis my men, I know I have to fight to the last. Being Catholic, I also know that God will protect me and help me to protect the young people under my command and it will not always be easy. I know because many of them have been turned into Nazi fanatics. They still believe in the final victory."

That is when I told him the story of my campaigns.

"Finally, Dr. Weber, allow me to deliver a thought that crossed my mind last night. The more I watched your guests the more I thought that I am witnessing the 'twilight of the Nazi Gods.' They say that Hitler likes the works of Wagner, but now it is for him to live his own twilight, but not as giant, certainly even less as a God, but as a bad gnome. Pardon my frankness, but I have nothing to lose. I think my war stories have bored you and, anyway, I must soon join my battalion."

"No! Think again! You are a young and very brave man. Your experiences and your military exploits in Italy captivated and surprised me. No one ever told it as you did. To be quite honest, the actual conditions under which our soldiers have to fight are not known to the top of the Party hierarchy. Thorsten was well advised to choose you to represent him. I thank you because I learned a lot."

We had a champagne lunch and then the driver took me back. I carried a package of groceries and a bottle of champagne from Madame Weber, for Thorsten and me to share. With a long kiss, I bade farewell to Marianne. On the train I had plenty of time to think about this unusual weekend and the unique opportunity to rub shoulders with a sample of the 'Nazi elite'. What would the reaction be in Zwickau?

I had told the Major of the time of my return and he sent for me immediately. Anton served us a schnapps and a beer and the Major went right to the heart of the matter:

"At the end of next week the majority of officers, NCOs and the new soldiers will join the Eastern front. First to Braunschweig where they will be equipped with the latest weaponry, then most likely to Danzig to form a new line of defense against the Red Army. I spoke with our SS Captain and told him that we need you here to supervise more military training. Incidentally, he wants to see you. It seems he has changed a bit. Want me to ask him for dinner with us tonight?"

- With pleasure! Besides, I have to give him a package.

- Anton will do that for you

At the SS Captain's place, the table was set.

- We'll have a cold meal with champagne. Charlotte has prepared a full meal.

- I guess Charlotte is Dr. Weber's wife?

- Yes, they are a lovely couple. Incidentally, Heiner was on the phone with me long time to tell me about your stay. He let me know your opinions and your insight on the current situation in Germany, but he also told me about your courage. He said that I can trust you totally.

During dinner the Captain confirmed that he has agreed with the Major to keep me in Zwickau until late November. Then came the great surprise: they had arranged for my enrollment in the officer school in Potsdam!

"You know, it's always a bit of a timing issue. Before 1942, the training of future officers took six months. Currently, it is three months, maybe even less. As for the training of recruits, the Major has already organized everything. Saturday I'm going to Plauen. I think I will be back on Monday or Tuesday, which will allow us to meet again before you leave. Until I return, if you want to call your family, you just use my secure private line."

- Thank you very much, Captain!

- Just call me Thorsten.

I wished him a good trip to Plauen and to thank the Webers again. He shook my hand. Yes, it was obvious, his mind set had indeed changed. Perhaps had I contributed to turning him in the right direction.

The next morning I turned to my correspondence. I will write a long letter to my parents and my sisters. What if it was the last memory they would have from me? If all went well, these letters would arrive in about eight days, just when I would leave

Zwickau. Of course, any attempt to project the future was uncertain.

The Major called. He wants to see me at noon. That would give me time to write.

Then he went on:

- All officers, NCOs and new soldiers are leaving tomorrow. We will say our goodbyes during dinner at the mess.

- I'll be there.

Everyone wanted to hear about my new assignments.

- I still have two weeks to complete the training of recruits and after that, only God knows.

- Why didn't you ask him? sneered the officer who believed in nothing.

- Because I love surprises!

The Major ordered a second round of beer and we sang together: 'This is a goodbye.' My heart was not in it.

Between recruit training and evenings out, the last days went fast. Lothar was no longer there to support me, I had no comrade who would stroll with me into town. I went alone. War widows were hungry, their ration cards had melted to next to nothing. I wanted to spend one last evening with a young widow of 24 years that I had befriended. I asked the Major whether our chef could provide me with enough extra food for a small meal. That's how I spent my last night in Zwickau.

On his return from Plauen, my SS Captain signed an order for his SS men to join their battalion. He said that the entire Weber family was sending their regards and best wishes, and then we talked about our future. Until further notice, he would remain in Zwickau. When the Red Army would approach, he would take refuge with the Webers.

- As for you, Heiner telephoned a friend in Potsdam to announce your arrival at the officer school, around December 1. Trains are now running very late, if at all.

Thanking Thorsten, I could not help but to find the situation rather unusual. Who would have thought that someday I would be recommended by an SS man? If I told this to my friends, they would think that I was kidding! Almost like reading my secret thoughts, Thorsten concluded:

- Tonight I'm meeting with the Major to resolve all the details. We will have dinner together. Still, what a change in so little time.

- Thanks for everything, Thorsten. You can confide in a young man of only 20 years because he believes in God.

The next day the Major told me that my marching orders were set for November 28 evening. He handed me my train ticket to Potsdam and the admission letter from the officer school with its full address and telephone numbers.

I asked Thorsten if I could use his direct line.

- Come tomorrow at half past twelve. My secretaries will be having lunch and will come back at 2pm. I will be away for at least an hour. You can then make your call in total privacy.

That's what I did. I had everyone on the line, including Josef. When I told him I was using the private line of an SS Captain there was silence.

- Are you pulling my leg?

- No, I'm alone in his office, there is absolutely no one to listen in. And I can spent a lot time on our phone call. You know, when you have the Good Lord by your side everything is possible. I leave in two days for the Potsdam officer school. After that, God only knows. But reassure our parents, I will return. Say hello to your commander.

- You really have a lot of nerve!

- No Josef, just the courage of my opinions.

On November 28, 1944, days before my 20th birthday, Thorsten accompanied me to the station in his SS uniform, shook my hand and said, "Good luck, Aloÿs!" I felt the tears fogging up my eyes. He looked at me one last time. I waved goodbye, and he disappeared into his car.

*

CHAPTER 9

Preparing to Lead Men into Battle

The train from Zwickau to Berlin moved slowly. In many places the bomb damaged road beds had barely been repaired. We passed through hopelessly sad landscapes under a murky sky, in rain and snow, typical for late November. The only good thing about this poor visibility was that we were protected from Allied air attacks.

On November 30th we arrive at Berlin Central Station. What a disaster! A ruined city, totally gutted. Only longtime Berliners could find their way around. Our War College was installed at the Bornstadt section of Potsdam, an area still relatively untouched by bombing, with its rococo style castle, Frederick the Great's famous "Sansouci".

At the College we are received by the administrative staff. The secretary examines my marching orders and my papers, "Colonel Kuehn, the school's commandant, would like to meet you as soon as possible." She adds thoughtfully: "You must have friends in high places." With that, she leads me to the Colonel's office. "Heil

Hitler!" The Colonel welcomes me and offers me a seat. He is around 50, ramrod straight, wears the Knight's Iron Cross, one of the highest honors, and a few other decorations. I could not help staring at it.

"This Cross you see me wear is the reward for the courage of my men. I came back from the 1914-18 war with the rank of captain. Reentering the Wehrmacht in 1933 as Major, I've trained many soldiers since. When we attacked Poland, along with the Russians, I was a battalion commander. After that, in the campaign in France as lieutenant colonel. I was wounded twice. Once in 1942 near Leningrad, the second time late 1943. My regiment fought with great courage, I lost many men. For me and many others the war was over. In 1944 I was appointed Commander of the War College and I think I will finish my career here, with the help of God. About the praise you received from your friends at Plauen: I remember something important. You did not hesitate to say loud and clear that you were a believer. This greatly impressed them! They said that you are a man we can trust."

"Colonel, I have never hidden my personal beliefs, nor betrayed anyone's trust. I'm only 20, with limited military experience, but I know that the worst is waiting for me. After our training here, I will be sent to a new regiment. Training and education of soldiers are for me crucial issues. Today much of Germany is a field of ruins but we have seen nothing yet. Dozens of generals, obeying a leader unable to lead the army still will send soldiers to be massacred, all while he is holed up in his bunker. Sir, please excuse my frankness, but there are so many thoughts we are obliged to keep to oneself, and one is tempted to open his heart when you feel confident to do so."

"Just between us, I can tell you that the battle of Stalingrad, the loss of the 6th Army and Hitler's obstinacy insisting that Paulus had to hold Stalingrad to the last man, all this has sown doubt among many officers regarding the much touted strategic 'genius' of the Führer and his staff. Now we all know better."

He gets up, shakes my hand and set another appointment for the next day. He calls for his secretary who leads me to my room:
- Have you known him a long time?
- I came here as a secretary early 1944 and he arrived in June. We women replaced all the men, except for our administrative chief, a sergeant, a fine guy like you. Except you are young and good looking.
- How old is he?
- 56 or 57, I think.
- How old are you, miss?
- I'm 21, but I have worked since I was 18 as a secretary in a private office.
- Very interesting. Can we meet again?
- With pleasure, looking at me with a smile. I am smitten.

I had to share my room with another sergeant. The room was well divided giving some semblance of privacy for each - a wardrobe, a bed and a desk with telephone, and a toilet.

My room mate, Wolfgang, had already been at the College for a week. He was 21, with the Iron Cross 2nd Class, along with a medal for his wounds. He was born in Westphalia, had been wounded in Belgium during an English surprise attack. After his recovery he joined his reserve battalion in Hanover and applied to become a career officer.

- You know, he says, the College Commander is a Colonel with the Knight's Cross, I was told he is very competent.
- We sure need someone competent for our training to be victorious in the final battle.
- You believe in the final victory?
- As much as you do.....

He does not know what to make of my reply. Whatever, it was time for dinner where he would introduce me to the other aspiring officers. The majority of them were my age. They were NCOs, some already lieutenants. Few of them had the Iron Cross 1st class.

The next morning we find ourselves in a large conference room. Four majors accompany Colonel Kuehn who immediately takes the floor and explains that the first part of the training will take place in this room. It will be a classical training to be followed by field training as part of a battalion under the command of one of the majors.

The Colonel then presents the four majors, all highly decorated. They were all in their thirties. Then the Colonel announces the appointment of twelve adjutant sub-lieutenants. I am one of them. The ceremony takes place immediately after the conference. We hand our uniform jacket to a tailor who, ten minutes later, brings them back with new shoulder tabs, two more silver bands for me.

Less than a month later, our theoretical training ends. On December 20 the colonel tells us that the College would be closed on the 31st. He added that in three days he would induct the new lieutenants, and on the 24th an Army chaplain would come to celebrate Christmas Mass in the conference room.

On December 23, 1944, I get my new uniform as lieutenant. I had barely turned twenty, and I am an officer! In addition, at the request of my commander at Zwickau, the Colonel gives me the war wounded medal. Wolfgang also was named lieutenant and he was very proud. On the 24th, we meet at the Christmas mass. To my surprise, almost everyone attends the service, including the colonel and three of the majors.

After Mass, we eat supper in our mess hall, and who comes to greet me? The secretary: "About our appointment, when is it?" I did not even know her first name - Erika. An hour later, I call her at her office. Laughter on the phone, they pass the telephone to her. She has two days off coming to her. Why not take a trip to Berlin? She has a small apartment she shares with a friend. Perfect. We will take the train tomorrow morning. Great - specially as the forecast is for bad weather - no bombing today.

War makes everything go upside down: now we are happy for bad weather.

A sunny day creates fear!

We walk through a devastated Berlin. The population survives in caves. Food is incredibly scarce and the biting cold spreads death among the hapless Berliners. On a demolished building there remaines a plaque: "Alexanderplatz", once the district of the elegant Berlin, famous around the world. I then remembered that in our school library I had seen a book called "Berlin-Alexanderplatz", by a certain Alfred Doblin. I promised myself that on my next visit home I will ask Mr. Unverzagt to tell me about it.

Erika and I take the way back to the apartment she shares with her friend Sophie. What does she do for a living? Her job is to issue food ration cards which gives her some contacts with the black market. Beware, hush, she should not talk about this. Before leaving, I promise Sophie to bring a friend next time, "to spend quality time together." We take the night train back to Potsdam. Erika goes back to her place at the reception. Wolfgang gives me a picture of our group of newly made lieutenants with the colonel.

- Thanks, Wolfgang, tomorrow when I write to my parents and I will send them this photo, perhaps the last, who knows!

- That's interesting, I wrote today thinking the same thing.

- We do not know our future. One thing is sure, we will have to face the raw power of the Red Army who will try to destroy us immediately.

To cut this gloomy atmosphere I ask Wolfgang if he had already eaten. No, he had waited for me. "Then let's go, it will lighten our rotten mind." The war does not let go of us, not even at meal time. Soon the conversation turns to our next training session that would be simulating the action of an attack regiment. Each battalion would be equipped with the terrible MG 42 machine guns, the assault rifle StG 44 and the new mortar 120. We would have extraordinary fire power but for how long? The ammunition supply is the number one problem!

The last days of 1944 pass quietly. I am writing letters and phone Clara. I give her my news about Berlin, she tells me the Fulda rail station was destroyed. Her brother Karl Heim was to report for military service on January 12th in Frankfurt-Oder. The Hünfeld train station and Hersfeld were also bombed.

On December 31st, the Colonel calls all officers together to announce that from now on all outside contact was forbidden. We receive our new military IDs. My marching orders are that our battalion would remain in the barracks. The Colonel confirms that the high command was determined to create an elite attack regiment equipped with ultramodern weapons. The infantry companies would receive a new type of bazooka that was said to be able to pierce the armor of the dreaded Russian T-34 tank. In addition, each battalion would have a company equipped with a new advanced design mortar. Every officer and NCO was issued a P38 pistol. Personally, I preferred the old 7.65 mm, which seemed not only more maneuverable but had bigger magazine than the P38.

- Any questions? I raised my hand:

- Colonel, I have two questions: does every officer here know how to handle these new weapons? Second, where will the soldiers be instructed and trained? I understand we have only four weeks.

- Two good questions. For the first, I think that all officers are fully instructed.

No problem with the MG 42, but only six officers were familiar with the StG 44!

Regarding the second question, the Colonel hesitated.

"We realize that we do not have many soldiers available to us. Some of them will come from reserve battalions. They have good military experience because they have already been in combat. Many of the others will be from the Home Guard, this is a group of older men between 50 and 60 years, and young fanatics between 15 and 16 years. They have only rudimentary weapons and little training. They are sent with you to the front to fill the ranks of depleted infantry divisions. The Home Guard is under the control of the local Party Chiefs, you know, the 'golden pheasants.'

I got the promise from Himmler, head of the High Command, that the Party Chiefs will not interfere in the operation of the attack regiment."

Our regiment has four battalions. Major Stauffer commands the first battalion to which I belong.

*

Between January 2 and 4 the recruits arrived. Each company had about eighty soldiers. As we did not have enough NCOs, the colonel ordered the majors to select the most qualified corporals to act as NCOs.

I needed two NCOs to complete my unit. I quickly looked for promising candidates. The two I selected were 22 years old, with good war experience; even after the end of the war, they wanted to continue their military career as NCOs. The remaining two corporals were content to stay in their rank. They made it clear that they wanted to stay close to their fellow soldiers. The oldest of my NCO choices, Corporal Schneider, was 26 years old with an Iron Cross 2nd class. He immediately inspired confidence. I thought that this one could be my future 'guardian angel'. He was married, had one child and came from a village near Münster in Westphalia. His simple ways reminded me of one of Jesus' parables: "The haughty shall be abased, and who humbles himself will be exalted." After observing him for a while I concluded that this man deserved a special effort to protect him. I shook his hand saying, I trust in you. Major Stauffer validated my choice:

- Major, I want Corporal Schneider to stay in my company. He suffered under the Nazi regime like my family did. I saw you at the midnight mass and I think you are Catholic.

- Indeed. The colonel told me about you, I hope to live to the end of the war with you, God willing.

I called my eighty new soldiers together to explain briefly the immediate course of action:

- Number one - Get your new winter outfit. All in white, helmet included. Keep warm.
- Second: Instruction and basic exercise.
- Third: Weapons training.

I asked the adjutants to tell their section to get their winter clothing. Next: Meeting tomorrow morning at 8 am for the first instruction session.

Meanwhile, snow had covered the Potsdam region, all of eastern Germany and our future battlefield further east. I went to bed thinking of my recruits.

January 5, 1945. For the first time, I had a company under my command! The Home Guard contingent wore their usual ragged uniforms, no camouflage. I welcome them to our new attack regiment, and then I continue:

"Our Führer is currently in Berlin in his bunker and directs our army to the final victory. According to my information, you are among the best of the Home Guard and you will be among those who will have the honor of defeating the Soviets and their powerful army. I hope you are convinced of our final victory."

All these half-baked soldiers respond in unison: "Of course, sir." I ask the platoon leaders to start with instructions on the use of our new weapons to a point where every soldier can use them with their eyes closed. "After that, we will do the first endurance exercise on the ground." I end my speech with a "Heil Hitler!" to which the recruits respond with great fervor. Then I organize a small meeting with our section heads to set the details of the program, stressing the need for a good breakfast because the exercises would last all day.

After the first day of endurance exercises the Home Guard recruits were on their knees, which did not prevent me to announce that the next training will be even harder. I then sensed the first signs of discouragement in their ranks. The recruits were beginning to find out that military life did not consist of a parade before their Party Chief......

Around the 20th of January, we begin with live ammunition shooting exercises. Again, I show them my attack technique. I never cease to harp on the topic of the final victory and it was good that I did. Indeed, a few days after the start of training, the Colonel had gathered the battalion and company commanders. He wanted to warn us confidentially that the Gestapo had infiltrated each Home Guard company.

Then the Colonel informed us that he would leave the regiment shortly. He had requested a transfer to a small garrison town near Hanover until the end of the war: "As you already have seen, the secretariat and reception are closed for four days. The old sergeant joined a Home Guard company in the east of Berlin. Before my departure I will introduce your new commander who will lead your regiment to the Central east front, probably in Silesia."

We continued our drills without stopping, day and night. In the evening, the soldiers were fed a very thick soup with bread and water. Barely asleep, an alarm and a 'counter attack' threw everyone out of bed, often until 5am. A little rest was granted and after coffee and a liverwurst sandwich we were going at it again. My little fanatics could no longer stand it, and the older ones would not even speak. Among them I think I located the Gestapo guy, and I'm sure I am not mistaken.

On January 27 the Colonel gets the battalion and company heads together to introduce his successor, Lieutenant Colonel Hausenberger, a Bavarian, 40-45 years, a huge man, almost seven feet, with a penetrating gaze, Knights Cross, Iron Cross 1st class, with an air of superiority. No doubt this lieutenant colonel is the man for the job to end this war. Colonel Kuehn introduced him to the battalion and company chiefs and officially handed him the command. We are now under his command. This ceremony went smoothly. Our former Colonel invites us to a beer. It's time to say goodbye to this great man.

Significantly, all this ceremony took place without a single "Heil Hitler!" The next day, Lieutenant Colonel Hausenberger brought this salute back and made it very clear that it was mandatory. He then formally presented the new name of our attack regiment: we are now officially Regiment 14. Tomorrow, on January 29th, the company commanders will make all soldiers ready for the front, make sure that they were getting their winter clothing ready for the bitter winter cold. Snow would accompany us on our train ride and welcome us on our arrival at the front.

Everything went as planned. On the set date, our regiment boarded the trains, each with a wagon for food, a field kitchen and two wagons for munitions.

A somber departure to an unknown future.

*

CHAPTER 10

Leading my Men into Battle

All the way from Berlin to Görlitz, snow is falling. A good thing: this was our assurance of not being attacked by Russian planes. As for the Allied bombers, I had the strange idea that they would no longer care to intervene.

Arriving in Görlitz, we unload the train as fast as we could. We load our reserve ammunition, the mortars and the field kitchens onto tracked vehicles and regroup by battalions. Trucks take us towards the city of Hirschberg but the last seven miles from the front we were unloaded to walk the rest. First stop: the city of Hirschberg, now a ghost town, deserted by its inhabitants. My friend Wolfgang is the head of the 2nd company. He and I walk side by side, in total darkness, other than the faint light of the moon through the clouds.

Suddenly, Wolfgang says, in all seriousness: Aloÿs, I know this place!

- What are you talking about? You were born in Westphalia, have you ever been in Silesia?

- No, never, yet I assure you, somehow I remember this city. Here, you'll see, at the next corner, there is a pharmacy.

Indeed, there is a pharmacy. It continues like that. Wolfgang anticipates all buildings: the Town Hall, the nearby small Catholic church, the Protestant church, everything is as he announces, except that everything lies in ruins. I begin to wonder. Wolfgang did not budge, he is certain to have known this city. Meanwhile, I told him to join his company, because we should not be late.

- Yes, you're right Aloÿs, we'll talk later.

I continued my walk alone, bewildered, thinking of the story of the city 'already known'. Fantastic stories based on inexplicable phenomena come up from my childhood. When adults began to speak of that I was always sent to bed. These stories always created a sense of insecurity and fear. I would sneak back, stealthily, my ear against the door to listen to adults. One day, I confessed to father Pralle. He confirmed that people in ancient times believed firmly that some of the dead had found a way to come back in an invisible form. As this good priest wanted to reassure me, he added that these 'ghosts' were not trying to hurt you. Shaking off my thoughts about the obscure I turned to my duties about a war that did not leave the slightest doubt about its reality!

A corporal sent by Major Stauffer ordered all company commanders to join him immediately. We found the Major and his staff in a house at the exit of the city where he was quartered. In a few sentences, he got us up to date on the situation:

- Our battalion is located two miles from 'coffin mountain', a hill that overlooks the entire region. Currently it is held by the Red Army. Tomorrow night we have to take that mountain at all costs and keep it as long as we can, because there are many civilians west of Hirschberg trying to flee the area. Is that clear?

The next day the weather was with us: gray and low clouds. The Russian planes would be grounded. My company had established its headquarters in a large building on the far side of Hirschberg. The other two companies were not far away, the battalion commander positioned in the middle, the canteen at 200 yards. That night, we had a good soup and army bread, water and hot coffee. Then everyone went to sleep. The night was freezing cold, but we were so exhausted that we slept well.

Upon awakening, after coffee, a meeting of the company commanders with the Major. We were shown a detailed map of the coffin mountain. It deserves its name. The Major details the plan of attack for the regiment. While our battalion will begin to climb the hill, a mortar battalion will cover our advance by targeted fire on the Soviet positions. "What do you think?" We look at the map, showing a near vertical drop of all its sides. I particularly focused on the downhill side of the Soviet front:

"Major, to avoid maximum casualties, I propose one company frontally attack the mountain, with a scouting group in front equipped with flare guns directing our mortar fire. We do not know if the Russians had placed mines to protect against a surprise attack. The other two companies will encircle the mountain and shut off the retreat of the Russians.

"Great idea, but the taking of the mountain is important. I will contact the head of the regiment for two additional companies as back-up and to make sure Russian reinforcements do not take you from behind. We will remain in telephone contact. Keep your operator near you."

At 6 o'clock, night fell. The Major issues a new call for a meeting in half an hour. Lieutenant Colonel Hausenberger will be present and other majors. He will present the battle plan for the next two weeks.

In this plan two battalions will be assigned to take over after the first attack and occupy the mountain. The surprise has to be total. One battalion will take up positions at the left and another at the right of the mountain to fight off surprise attacks and one battalion will remain in reserve near the regiment headquarters. All planned moves were plotted on a large map of the terrain. The Lieutenant Colonel concludes:

Set your watch: it's exactly 6.55pm. At 10pm exact we launch the attack. Leave your gas masks behind. You'll get a good meal, the chef has prepared for each of you a bread with sausages.

Remember to fill your water bottles. For the rest, listen to your company commander.

At 9:50, my company is in place. Half an hour earlier, I told a section head to take care of my men to give me time to survey the terrain in front of us with a sergeant and my "guardian angel", Corporal Schneider. I especially wanted to see the land behind the mountain. To move fast in the deep snow we were on skis. No trace of the Soviets. At 9:55 we were back. I give the order to a section chief to advance with twenty-five men to within half a mile from the supposed Russian line. They were to cover us in case of a surprise counter attack.

The twenty-five men left, my company is now reduced to fifty soldiers. To our left is Wolfgang's company, on the right that of Heinrich. At ten we launch the attack. I had the strong feeling that the Russians had positioned themselves on top of the mountain, that is to say right before us. Halfway through our advance, I order a stop and complete silence. I went ahead accompanied only by a sergeant and my Corporal Schneider. We have a small bazooka and some hand grenades with us. Climbing silently as possible, we hear a noise. We move cautiously ahead until we hear the voice of Russians. They talk quietly, they feel safe. I send my NCO to inform the other companies and ask Lieutenant Wolfgang to contact Major Stauffer to inform him of what I found and of our intention to launch a surprise attack with our three companies at midnight. It seemed to me that the plateau is sparsely occupied since the Russians feel they are control of the situation.

Alas, the Heinrich company imprudently arouses the attention of the enemy. At 11:45pm. the Russians opened fire. In an attempt to relieve some of the company, I get closer and closer to the Russian camp and give orders to my sergeant to shoot his bazooka on their fortified position. For my part, I decide on a sort of bunker twenty yards ahead of me.

Both explosions cause some disarray among our opponents. I shout "Charge!" and we spray the first line of the Russians with deadly assault rifle fire and hand grenades. Those who were inside their shelter come out and in turn strafe us with their Kalashnikovs. There must be at least a battalion confronting us, and they are well armed. In the dark of the night, between the trees, enemies and friends we are in confused combat. We advance by shooting anything that moves. With twenty men I reach the first Russian line seeing them recede, destabilized. Suddenly, out of nowhere, two Russian soldiers stand in front of me, aiming at me and are mowed down with an assault rifle. My 'guardian angel' has just saved my life! Corporal Schneider, thank you! We press on with the assault to maintain our advantage.

Wolfgang and his company are in full attack from the right. The Soviets feel caught in the middle and retreat toward the center of their camp. The battle becomes increasingly bloody.

From our side we call for stretchers and medics. I feel a burning along my arm, not the time to think about it! We mercilessly roll back the Russians. Suddenly, flares from the plateau. Our troops have reached the top and have repulsed the enemy. The bazookas are not idle, their explosions spread panic, and so do our hand grenades. On either side there are dead and wounded, but at 5am we see our victory. The Russians come out of their positions, hands in the air. An officer comes forward, he holds a white flag and tells us in a quite understandable German that his battalion surrenders.

I phone to Major Stauffer to give him an update, adding that it is still dark and it is therefore difficult to disarm the Russians. He replied that he will join our company immediately from the other side with his men and that he will send a battalion to prevent the rest of the Russians from escaping. During that telephone conversation, the Russian officer remained immobile, twenty feet in front of me. I asked the other officers to lay down their arms but they hesitated. At this time, from the side of the 3rd Company, some one opened fire again on the Russians. The result is terrible. For twenty minutes, it's a slaughter. The Russians are surrounded, we hear their orders to cease-fire. Their survivors come out of their positions, with their hands up, unarmed.

The day finally rises, the sky is clear, one can now see the extent of the disaster. Major Stauffer joined us and said that on the other side of the mountain there were only about twenty Russians and an officer. When our company surprised them they surrendered without any resistance.

We begin to disarm the Russian soldiers, one after the other. Then we walk them down the mountain to be taken over by the 2nd Battalion. Thirty prisoners remain with us to collect the dead and bury them in hastily dug graves. The bizarre behavior of one of their wounded attracts my attention. This is a Russian soldier who moves with great difficulty from one grave to another, and blessed the dead by brandishing a cross. When he has finished, he falls to his knees and looks up to the sky in prayer. Something overcomes me, I rush to him give him my support. His open eyes seem to stare at me, but they are far away, like looking into eternity, like he communicates with heaven. I give him a sign of the cross on the forehead and pray, "God Almighty will lead you to eternal life." His head collapses suddenly. He is dead. It was then that I realized that half his arm was torn off. It must have taken him an incredible effort to go from grave to grave. A young Russian soldier approaches and makes me understand that he would bury the priest. We both are lowering him in a pit with four others. The soldier puts the cross on his chest. Then he covers everything with a mixture of earth and snow red with blood.

I asked the Russian officer who confirmed that an Orthodox priest did belong to their battalion. Very few officers and soldiers knew. In the Soviet army any presence of a religious would have brought terrible reprisals by the most powerful man in their battalion: the political commissar representing the Communist Party. "Where is he in this hour, your commissar?" According to the officer, he is certainly among the other prisoners, probably having removed his insignia so that he would go unnoticed. "Could you recognize him?" "Of course!" Then, turning to the major, the Russian officer requests permission to put a bullet between that man's eyes.

At the very least, the Russians had lost half of their battalion. We had to take inventory of our own losses. My company had lost four men and had twelve wounded. The soldiers I had sent behind the coffin mountain were retracing their steps when they understood that the offensive was launched. No loss on their side.

The third company, under the command of Heinrich, was destroyed. They stood on my right, but without warning a young Hitler Youth of the Home Guard had opened fire against the Russian position, triggering a rapid response. Heinrich was killed instantly, plus a sergeant, a platoon leader and two NCOs and most of their front line. Later, it was again the third company that had opened fire indiscriminately. Same scenario but worse. The snow was turning red. In total, by the mere lack of discipline of some young fanatics, the third company had lost thirty six men, and fourteen were injured.

In Wolfgang's 2nd Company six soldiers were killed and nine wounded. Fortunately, I must say, our medics were very efficient. The stretcher-bearers went in there quickly to take the wounded for first aid. The dead were taken away in trucks towards Hirschberg for a military burial.

Meanwhile, the sun rose on a clear sky. The immediate consequence was a Russian plane flying over the mountain plateau which houses all prisoners. Concentrated at the foot of the mountain part of our forces were hidden from the aircraft. Then other planes came to bomb and strafe the prisoners until none were left alive. History has taught us that Stalin considered any of their soldiers that were taken prisoner as traitors or deserters, to be executed by firing squad.

It was time for me to address an issue that concerned me at the highest level. I asked Major Stauffer to question the head of the 3rd Company, the only warrant officer or head of section still alive, to clarify some points.

The Lieutenant Colonel was waiting in his headquarters in the former town hall of Hirschberg. I was the only company leader, surrounded by the four majors. On seeing me, immediately

Hausenberger expresses his astonishment by an unfriendly frown. Stauffer takes the lead:

"Colonel, we are here at the request of Lieutenant Aloÿs Pappert. If we have overcome the Russians it is largely thanks to him and his combat experience. We would like to understand why we were sent to Hirschberg and why some one gave orders to shoot at the Russians after they had already surrendered. We learned by interrogating a Russian officer that only one Soviet battalion was still in the area."

The silence that followed made each one of us guess the truth:

"In the army, we receive orders and execute them. You do not know the supreme commander of the Army Group Centre, General Ferdinand Schörner. I wish you will never meet him. The Hirschberg order came directly from him. He set a trap to his direct opponent, Marshal Konev. Konev and several infantry divisions were involved in an earlier breach. Schörner surrounded the Russians. The battle raged. He asked me to come to his aid with a Home Guard regiment of the 78th Division. It was Schoerner's own personal ambition to show off to his Russian adversary that made him give the Hirschberg orders."

The snow begins to melt but there is still enough of it to make it difficult to move during the day. Never fire on a Russian aircraft. We have two days to reach the 78th Division. Cars with the dead and wounded will move only at night, towards Dresden. We leave Hirschberg at 3am. Our chef has prepared a solid soup and sandwiches and for each a little tart.

At 3am we break camp and walk all day. In the evening, two hours of break. We are exhausted, we throw ourselves on the sides of the road to sleep, anywhere, anyhow. I try to swallow a sandwich. It seems to me that I have to stay awake at all costs so that my company will have someone leading it. So, to give me some courage I go to see Stauffer, and I find him not far from a truck with the wounded. He offers me a glass of brandy before we take care of my arm and he leads me to the doctor. The physician, still quite young, examines my wound: a bullet went through the arm without touching the bone. This time, the bitter cold is a good thing because it helped prevent a nasty infection. After his care, we go back to our units. Passing the Major's area, a simple tent, he serves me a hot coffee. We must start our march again. All men are sleeping. I wake two section chiefs, two NCOs and my 'guardian angel'. They have difficulty waking from sleep, unable to open their eyes.

"Rub your eyes with a little snow and get up! Wake the others, we must leave. From now on, no more breaks. Here's how you organize the march. You'll march by threes, the middle one will be supported by the other two and will be allowed to sleep while you are walking. Then you change place. In this way six hours of walking, everyone has had two hours of sleep. Every NCO is responsible for his group. I will keep walking past you to check."

Not that easy to wake up all these zombies! Some soldiers protest, they are too tired. One of them even said that he would rather die here than elsewhere later in a few days. I approach him, pull my gun and shoot two fingers above his head. He screams in fright and jumped into the ranks. Wolfgang, passing by, thinks it is an excellent method....

So we went for a 'long walk'. Fatigue ended up winning me over, too. I was reminded of our exercises in the time of the training of young recruits: a marching song! That's what we need! I start to sing. Immediately, this initiative is spreading. While they all start to sing, I set the speed with "a two, one-two" for a very steady pace. The lungs expel fatigue, replaced by fresh air. The company gets out of its torpor. I gather all my strength. Wolfgang does the same. Only old soldiers of the Home Guard balk. Knowing that among them there are Gestapo guys, I take them on their own propaganda:

"The final victory asks everyone for superhuman efforts. We have no other choice. We are not far from the 78th Division. They are counting on us."

The third company, now placed under the command of a warrant officer, follows by applying the simple rule: "March!"

Our march was, however, not so fast that it prevented us from seeing everywhere dead civilians who were killed trying to flee the Red Army. Women, elderly, children were lying on the side of the road, with their carts pulled by horses. Against them, Russian aircraft had not used only bombs but also machine guns. Maybe there were survivors amid all those bodies? No time to check. The sight of these unfortunate ones raised in me a mixture of feelings: impotence and hatred against Hitler and all those who had helped to transform Germany into a huge field of ruins. I swore to myself I will not leave any opportunity to remove a Nazi, including the Gestapo that had infiltrated my unit. The time would come soon when they would have less and less power. At least that is what I thought.

Next day we were able to link up with the 78th Division. The Americans and British had bombed Dresden on the nights of February 13 to 14. Stalin, however, who was closer to the city did not make a move. I also found that the Russians had not bombed bridges or roads or railways, a military strategy that seemed relevant.

General Ferdinand Schörner was promoted to Field Marshal by a special decree of the Führer. The same day he sent an order to all division commanders to require that the military would henceforth make the salute "Heil mein Führer!"

The battle of Bautzen-Görlitz was far from over. For two weeks, we harassed the Red Army to eliminate pockets of resistance. The majority of Soviets had managed to escape and, therefore, many dispersed units put up a fierce resistance. The Russian aviation was grounded because of bad weather, just as the German air force which was non existent. The battle was often fought on a small area of just one square mile.

Towards the end of February, our battalion had encircled an area of several villages where the Russians were trapped. According to Major Stauffer, it would be very difficult to dislodge them. I then offered to break through in the center, while the 2nd company would attack from the left and the third from the right. It would take an additional company to cut the Russians' escape route so that they would not be fighting us again. Stauffer promised to take care of the necessary arrangements.

To facilitate the attack, we put our mortars into action. We took the first village at the end of a fierce battle. The ground was littered with Russian dead. What a horror! Women aged 12 to 80 watching us, crying, bewildered with terror in their eyes, bordering on madness! A week with the presence of the Red Army had meant the systematic rape of women and girls, along with the murder of the aged. An old woman led me to a barn door to which their priest had been nailed. I ask two soldiers to take the body of the martyr down before undertaking the systematic clearing of the village, house by house. With rage in our heart it was difficult not to kill every Russian that we flushed out in spite of the order by Marshal Schörner not to take any prisoners.

Schörner was a brutal man who imposed an iron discipline. Woe to the soldiers who, for one reason or another, had lost contact with their combat unit. They were immediately sentenced to death without a trial and hanged on a tree with a sign on his chest: 'I am a traitor'.

*

The fighting was very costly with so many men killed in action, in particular, the soldiers of the Home Guard who lacked experience and the stamina to save themselves. As for ammunition, our reserves were running out and I ordered the platoon leaders to limit the supply of ammunition per man.

Following the bombing of Dresden the rail links had become unusable. We were running out of everything, especially soldiers. Major Stauffer could only confirm:

"I will speak directly to the colonel. In the meantime I have bad news for you. Tomorrow night your entire company will evacuate to the area towards Dresden. The Dresden Party Chief asked us to send aid to clear the city. Our division, plus the rest of Army

Group Centre under the high command of General Schörner, will continue to push back the Red Army. Then we will hold our positions as long as we are able. According to our information, most divisions of the corps of Marshal Konev, including his aircraft were directed toward Berlin. You should return here no later than 10 March."

On the road to Dresden, always the same horrific scenes: horses, women, children, the old, tangled corpses, machine-gunned to death in their makeshift carts. At dawn, thousands of refugees crowded the road. Unable to move forward, Dresden remained out of reach. Forced to stop our column, I try to speak with someone in charge. No answer. Then a man calls me to talk to him. He is the mayor of a village nearby. It's citizens fled to escape the Red Army. I tell him to go back to his village. His area will remain German even if the Red Army occupies it.

- You are sure of what you say? Sure my town will remain German?

- Calm youself, I have my information. Anyway, you cannot go further.

From the corner of my eye, I noticed that the Gestapo guy was nearby every time I spoke to someone. I gave a discrete sign to my 'guardian angel', that he would monitor him closely, especially when we were in Dresden.

I divide my company into smaller sections and we briskly walk the last few miles. Entering the city, the horror of the bombing became clear to us. Everything was burned. Very few houses were still standing, even in the outskirts. Parts of the city's great promenades had been reopened for traffic, after bulldozers had cleared the rubble.

We had not yet reached the center when a commando of the SS and some 'golden pheasants' stopped us. I introduce myself, showing my marching orders and give all the information they wanted. "Oh, a full company! exclaimed the deputy prefect, how many men do you have?"

"Sixty-three in all and we hope that there will be reserves here." No answer.

One of the SS men leads us towards the center of the city. I see the Dresden Party Chief in conversation with an SS officer: "Hey! Aloÿs! Happy to see you again!" It's Thorsten! We shake hands warmly and he presents me to the Party Chief, at first rather friendly. I did not want to stay away from my company any longer.

- Where should we go to help?

- Don't worry, an SS officer will guide you there and you can join your company later.

With Thorsten we pick up the thread of our earlier conversations: "In the train from Plauen to Dresden, there are constant controls, the military police seeking deserters and escaped prisoners, or regular police checking civilians. I, in SS uniform, settled in a first class compartment and I was left alone. Werner, the Party Chief who helped me in Leipzig, was then appointed to Dresden, a city that until now had not suffered any bombing. One of the most beautiful cities in Germany! All gone now. It's still bizarre that Stalin had not moved in, his army is just a day away. How did it happen that the Allied did the bombing of Dresden when the Russians were already at the city's door steps? According to Werner, on the nights of February 13 to 15, between 1000 and 1500 bombers destroyed the city in three raids. The Red Cross estimated 350,000 deaths, mostly near the train station where more than 500,000 refugees were jammed into a small area. And since the city had no air defences the Allied hardly lost a plane!"

- As my father always said, we reap what we sow.

Thorsten did not respond, and for good reason. To talk about something else, I asked for news of Marianne and her parents.

- They're all fine. Besides, I am already registered in Bavaria at their address. And maybe I'm going to marry Marianne soon.

- Congratulations! Very good idea, but be quick. In two months the war may be over. For me, the future is a big question mark.

Even if the Russians take me prisoner, I will get out, I'm sure. Kiss our friends of Plauen, I will not forget you.

With that, I left Thorsten and I joined my company. Crossing this charred city, it gave off a burning smell that choked you, and I thought of the criminal nature of this bombardment. Perhaps the command of the Anglo-American air force had wanted to impress the Russians?

I found my men. They were searching for survivors together with civilians and the Red Cross. Doctors and nurses were providing first aid. Water trucks were dispensing water to these unhappy victims, often atrociously burned. Elderly men and women from the country side had been mobilized in large numbers. I felt that our presence in Dresden was useless and I gave order to regroup.

When they were all accounted for, we left the city toward the East. Only moving at night we finally found our regiment on March 9th. The Colonel had Hausenberger take command of our regiment. "The 78th Division? Taken over by General Nagel, a friend of General Schörner." We took this in without comment. We understood.

The Colonel had a hot meal prepared for us. We should rest because the next day we would find ourselves at the front, a few miles away. After the meal, I had a talk with my 'guardian angel' asking for news of the Gestapo:

"When he saw the welcome you received by the SS leaders and the Dresden Party Chief he was speechless. He asked if you knew all the dignitaries of the Party?" I replied, of course, and many others.

- Lieutenant, I do not think you will remain with us for long!

In the meantime, however, we have to face the prospect of another day of battling the Red Army.

*

CHAPTER 11

"War is Hell"
William Tecumseh Sherman

We are getting ready to go to the front. Surprise: On that bright morning over a hundred new soldiers come to join our troupes - a sad looking contingent from the Home Guard. As usual, they are the old men, 50 to 60 years, accompanied by very young recruits of just 16. One of these 'fighters' was barely 15. Another surprise: our Gestapo guys have disappeared. It seems that their order had come from above. It just means the former Gestapos have been replaced by some newcomers. At least we knew the former ones, now we have to start again finding the new Gestapo that could have infiltrated anywhere.

My company now had seventy-five men. I wanted to check out the new arrivals, together with my NCOs and with Corporal Schneider.

The young ones, real fanatics, had volunteered. One of the kids came from Brunswick near Hanover. His father owned a sugar factory that was bombed. I always concluded my interview with this question: "So you joined our battalion to participate in the final victory?" Answer is unequivocal: "Yes sir, Lieutenant".

With the older, the responses were less categorical. There were some genuine volunteers among them, but also 'court appointed volunteers', in other words, forced to enlist under dubious circumstances, unable to find other places in the reserves.

I also wanted to know their level of military training. The response of the youngest said it all: "I was ordered to show up in the barracks and given a uniform and a gun, without ammunition. Then I climbed into a truck that had brought me here. That's all". Ditto for the others. What are we to do with these guys?

Leaving these new 'fighters' in the care of my NCOs and Corporal Schneider, I go to see Major Stauffer, finding him in a meeting with Colonel Hausenberger. The way they look at me told me that the situation is very serious. The 78th Home Guard division cannot hold out much longer. The colonel telephoned General Schörner who gives us no more than a week to train the young recruits. In the meantime a Tiger Panzer Division will hold back the Red Army.

With this short time frame we must get organized fast. We gather our battalion, and I propose a program based on these points:

- What are our reserves of arms and ammunition?

- Given the short time we have we must start their training at an intense pace.

- We will continue our exercises until midnight every day.

- In one week, they must have acquired the basic skills for combat.

Good that we had been able to keep the weapons of our dead and wounded - we can give them to the new soldiers.

A week later, our new 'fighters' had lost a lot of weight, but gained muscle. They were exhausted. How much did they learn about their weapons?

*

The last night before going to the front we serve them a good soup. At midnight we will get on the way. I meet the company for a last message:

"Comrades, tomorrow morning we may be in combat. Every soldier must strictly obey the orders given by the platoon corporals and the NCOs. In two months the war will be over. Perhaps you will be dead or wounded. With God's help, I will do my best to keep you alive. We will never abandon our wounded. We will retreat only if your company commander gives the order. No one but we have the right to give you that order. Is this clear?"

An old Home Guard soldier then raises his hand:

- Lieutenant, I do not believe in God and in addition, I want to tell you that the war will be over only after our final victory.

- I did not say anything different: victory in two months at the latest.

Silence. There remained two hours of rest. Then we started to walk the six miles to the front lines, a walk in darkness, over muddy roads, to the sounds of the approaching battle. My Corporal Schneider whispers: "The Gestapo guy, the one who said he did not believe in God ..." He had swallowed the bait of my little sentence: "In two months the war is over" and thus was discovered. Let's monitor him closely ...

*

It was the week before Easter when we have our first contact with the Red Army. Once our regiment joined the 78th Division we launch our attack. The Russians occupied the nearby hills, holed up in the woods, away from the towns. I thought we could not be very far from the Czech border but we weren't sure. The uncertainty as to our exact position made me uncomfortable. I wished we had a good road map of the region.

Our battalion is given orders to cross a wooded area to establish contact with the enemy. We are spotted and run into a barrage of machine gun fire, and then artillery and tanks - everything.

Unable to fight back effectively we quickly retreat. Already a few of my men have died and some weapons are destroyed. The battalion commander gives the order to dig six positions with MG 42s on the edge of the woods. Objective: retrieve the wounded and collect the name tags of those who had not survived.

We now create a new line of defense about a mile from the woods, on a hill overlooking the plain. With Wolfgang's 2nd company we take over a big quarry. We begin to dig bunkers, cover them with tree trunks. We set up MG 42 machine-gun posts all around the perimeter and a battery of six inch mortars. Major Stauffer comes to inspect and tells us to dig fox holes everywhere. He recommends that we never show ourselves during daytime, use maximum camouflage. Two companies are placed left and right of our quarry to avoid encirclement at night. We are in an advanced position. The bulk of the regiment is a mile behind us.

- Will you allow me to scout with a group of four men to see what is happening on the other side of the woods?

- Why risk lives now? The war will be over in a few weeks.

- Major sir, we should not remain in this uncertainty. I want to know what might be happening. I will do my best to avoid a confrontation with the Russians. Tonight the moon is not very bright. I suggest we start at 9pm and, in principle, at midnight I'll be back. Our patrol will be armed with assault rifles, three hand grenades and a bazooka. God will be with us.

At 9pm I go ahead with two NCOs and Corporal Schneider. They are seasoned men.

Spring has arrived. The plain smells of fresh grass and flowers.

We enter the woods, getting used to the dark. We cautiously move forward until I hear a noise. Stop. Silence. Nobody moves. A Russian patrol passes ten yards ahead from us. They speak loudly, seemingly unconcerned. When they have passed we continue to move forward. Arriving at the edge of the woods a huge camp come in our view. Trucks, tanks, apparently the infamous T-34, soldiers chatting, everything perfectly in place - apparently a whole division.

This is enough for this reconnaissance mission. We turn back without the Russian patrol having noticed our presence. Before midnight we're back and I immediately made my report. I think the Russians will attack after Easter. Until then, they would harass us with mortar or artillery to gauge our defense. I ask the major to get me a map and, if possible, a compass.

Today is Friday, and I really want to walk to the nearby village to find some food. I ask Wolfgang for a few men to come with me.

- How many?

- Four, in addition to my own.

At headquarters, the Major grants me permission and gives me the map and the compass. A look at the map tells me that we are about 50 miles from the Czech border. The army corps in the centre of our line focuses its troops on Czechoslovakia. Schörner with his staff is still behind us, but for how long?

We quickly enter the village. I divided the team to check out four farms and some houses. Rally in half an hour near the church! Always accompanied by my Corporal Schneider, I choose the house of the priest. It is not locked. We go down into the basement with a kerosene lamp. Just what I had expected! There are potatoes, jams and three boxes of white wine, thirty-six bottles, plus some bottles of local beer. Good hunting for us scouts! What a welcome addition to our meager rations! We are back before 5pm, loaded like mules.

Saturday passes quietly when, at the time we were waiting for the food squad, a burst of mortar fire hits us. "Everyone take cover!" I throw myself into a fox hole, although the shots are not accurate a few shrapnel hit me, one of them in the jaw. We have three wounded. Helped by our first aid men, I make myself a bandage to stop the bleeding. I commandeer a truck, load the two seriously injured and give orders to my first platoon chief to take over command of my company until I return.

An emergency hospital had been set up some five miles behind our lines in the town hall. It is woefully insufficiently equipped. We must get to a military hospital with a Red Cross ambulance.

A doctor examines me, apologizing for not having anything for local anesthesia to remove the piece of shrapnel. I hear a crack and he shows me the small piece of metal, disinfects the wound, makes a bandage. I lie down on a makeshift bed. The pain was hard to take but in spite of it I fall sleep. I am awakened to take a painkiller to help end the pain. I go back to sleep.

It seemed to me that if I stayed in that hospital, I would die, and besides the food was terrible. I ask the head doctor to give me permission to rejoin my company. In principle, he has no right to let me out so fast and he makes me sign a waiver. "You have to be crazy to leave a military hospital voluntarily!"

Before leaving I visited the company wounded to remind them when leaving the hospital to get their marching orders stating our regiment number. Above all, never take a step outside without these documents!

Then I thanked the doctor and asked if there was a truck that was going in my direction. Luckily there was one, but it drops me after a few miles, continuing in another direction. Start walking! I start singing. What a road! A page out of the Dark Ages, marked by gallows and soldiers hanging from trees, humiliating panels hanging on their torsos.

Suddenly I hear an engine noise. A big Mercedes and two jeeps lumber up. I signal them to stop. The first vehicle stops for me. A gruff military policeman: "Your papers!" I hold out my marching order and all my documents. He examines everything and decides to show them to someone in the Mercedes while the other policeman keeps me under close watch. I ask him, "Are you perhaps Russians?" His response, a look of disgust and hatred. I forge ahead:

"Who is in this Mercedes? I want to know!"

The car door opens and a General in full regalia emerges. I click my heels and salute him with a "Heil Hitler, sir!"

"I'm Field Marshal Schörner and if I understand right you are on your way back to your unit. What is your regiment?" I give him all the details. He invites me to accompany him to the next village: "You have ten more miles to walk. But tell me, why did you leave the military hospital so early, your wound is still bleeding under your dressings".

- Field Marshal, sir, at the hospital I was starving. I prefer whatever little food we have at the front, but at least I can share it with my men.

Without further comment, Schörner tells me to get in the car with the policemen. At first the two soldiers are aghast. Then one of them whispers to me that the Marshal was impressed by my audacity. The ice is broken, a conversation begins, without showing me any sign of sympathy.

- You're not ashamed to hang these poor guys from a tree with this insulting panel on their chest?

- We just execute the sentences from the military court. They are just a few hundred yards behind us.

- In effect the orders are given by Field Marshal Schörner?

- Of course. He in turn executes the orders of our Führer Adolf Hitler.

End of this disheartening dialogue, and the end for me in this macabre motorcade. They drop me on the side of the road. Well, well, well, I just have met our supreme commander, Hitler's executioner ...

A week had passed since I left the hospital. My unexpected return creates a surprise, beginning with that of Major Stauffer who is very happy to see me. Wolfgang joins us. I tell them my story from A to Z, they cannot believe their ears. The Major wonders whether I would accompany him to meet with colonel Hausenberger. Of course!

The colonel had his headquarters in a village a few miles from our quarry. I did not know this ranking officer very well but obviously major Stauffer must have been singing my praises. The colonel had been made aware of my injury and, like others, was astonished that I had come back so soon. He expected me to give him a detailed account of my meeting with Schörner. I did not hide my feelings about the Marshal, his callous court martials and the hanging of soldiers that had been separated from their units most of them through no fault of their own. I went even so far as to tell them how disgusted I was with their callous ways.

- Everything like that is worth hearing, especially about your meeting with Schörner.

- Colonel, I will be happy to continue this conversation but only after getting something to eat because my stomach has been empty for days. They bring me a good meal and a beer.

- Colonel, do you know Marshal Schörner personally?

- Yes, I met him when I was given command of the 7th Division. I do not think I made a good impression on him because I was soon after replaced by Major General Nagel, a Nazi like him. But all this stays between us, gentlemen. Schörner's ears are everywhere!

- Sir, one more question: do you know where the Americans are at this time?

- They have already taken Hesse and parts of Bavaria.

A clear night sky with thousands of bright stars greet me on my return, a dream setting for peace. This eery silence, however, was telling me something:

- Major, sir, I think we need to put our regiment on alert. I believe that early tomorrow morning the Russians will attack. I have seen that they have a whole armada massed on the other side of the forest. I hope that our division is ready to hold them back. And believe me, this time we will fight until the end of the war running backwards.

The Major was not convinced by what he regarded as a mere hunch. I tried to convince him by recounting my experience with the Allied assault on Monte Cassino that had been preceded by the same deceptive calm.

"I am convinced that the Russian infantry is already now at the edge of the forest, or will be there in a few hours, and advance before dawn to surprise us. I propose that at about 2 am a machine gun opens fires into the edge of the woods. If the Russians are there, we will see a reaction. It is important that our quarry positions are not discovered. If we are attacked we will be better placed to respond from there because we control the plain before us."

The Major could not make this decision without the colonel's consent. With his agreement, he gave the green light. I had been successful in convincing him and I sent a prayer that my initiative would be good! I prayed inwardly, fervently. Intrigued, the Major watched my visible concentration. He looked at me with an expression of amazement. Answering his look, I told him that I was thinking of my father.

At 2am, according to my plan, one of our MG 42s begins to spray its bullets into the forest. Wolfgang is at my side as we note the immediate response from the Russians. Immediately the Major calls me:

- Aloÿs, you were right! Their offensive probably begins this morning. I'll inform the colonel.

- I hope we still have our tanks, artillery and the 88 cannons?

- The tanks were redirected to the Czech front, but we still have the means to stop the advance of the Soviets.

- May God hear you!

- The Major calls you by your first name? Wolfgang is surprised.

- It may be that from now on he takes my suggestions seriously. Listen, my dear Wolfgang, pray to God that we will be alive tonight, and together.

Both companies are ready for the assault, positioned impeccably. Wolfgang and I watch the ground. Before us, the enemy infantry had begun to advance slowly in a row a mile wide. Suddenly, on either side of the forest, the first tanks show up. The Russian infantry starts to storm toward our lines, screaming. Our MG 42s and our mortars cover the ground. Russian mortars fighting back, followed by their artillery.

The Russians did not expect our firepower from the quarry. Their artillery is also deadly. I run from one machine gun nest to the other: "Watch your ammo! Make every shot count! Same with the StG 44!"

The Russian tanks reach our hilltop positions. Horror! They pass over the fox holes where we had positioned our gunners. They stop their tanks and turn left and right to crush our soldiers. Simultaneously the tanks shoot at anything that moves. These are the dreaded T-34, fast, strong and deadly. Our soldiers are fighting back with bazookas, setting three of the tanks ablaze. The others continue crushing our comrades, turning them to mush. They were then attacked by two of our armored vehicles, equipped with the famous 88 cannons. Each shot finds its mark. The T-34s turn back. They lost twenty of them. A group of fighter-bombers flew over us but decide to attack the villages where most of our division is grouped.

We are finally able to repulse the Russian attack. Several T-34 are burning, the rest retreat. Our gunners continue firing into the woods, blindly, without the help from our surveillance aircraft. Our ammunition depot has to be moved because of a very strong explosion nearby with a huge column of smoke rising into the sky. In the distance, other black smoke columns signal that our positions were attacked by Russian planes.

All into the evening, the Russian artillery harassed us. At nightfall, the regiment retreats to a new line of defense six miles behind. We record the identity of the dead without taking their ID plates. The major asks us to dig a mass grave and bury the soldiers putting their helmets over their name plates.

My company loses five dead and seven wounded, four dead in Wolfgang's and eight wounded. Unfortunately, our Gestapo guy got away. We bury the unfortunate souls, saying a final prayer. Weapons and ammunition recovered, we leave this sad scene.

*

During the assault of the Russians I was horrified by how the T-34 had ground our living soldiers to mush. Conclusion: never have a defensive line without anti tank protection. That's for later. The immediate need is another night march. Dawn finds us in a wooded area. We turn south in the direction of Czechoslovakia. The day begins. The Major and I quickly inspect the field. The area is covered with clusters of big trees that make it impossible for the Russian tanks to get through. We place our companies into these forests. The terrain in front of us is easy to monitor. Major sends a platoon to the nearby village to get food to tide us over until our country kitchen is operational.

I give the order to dig new positions for our MG 42s, and trenches for four men each, armed with StGs 44 and bazookas, all inside the wooded areas. The mortar positions are behind the tree clusters for better visibility.

Another cloudless blue sky. Suddenly, an infernal noise: three strange looking planes showing the swastika are flying over us. These are aircraft without propellers, with some sort of canisters under the wings that seem to breathe fire. Major Stauffer knows more. What we have seen are a new type of jet planes, the first in the world, the Messerschmitt Me 262. He tells me that our pilots prefer propeller aircraft, they are easier to maneuver. They were so difficult to fly that some of them had crashed. If we can believe Stauffer, some of their pilots even had fled and delivered their planes to the Allied.

Walking with him to inspect our new defense lines I explained the position of my men. He advised me to place three mortars behind the woods with only four shells to a mortar. The day before, the Russian air force had hit an ammunition depot. No more ammunition reserves and already in mid-April ... How long can we hold the Russians back?

- Have you identified your Gestapo man?
- Not yet.

- Pity. I know mine and I gave him a pleasant surprise. It is he who will hoist the flag tomorrow before dawn with orders to stay next to the flag, with his arm raised in the Hitler salute. If you want my advice, just after hoisting the flag, quickly withdraw your company to the interior of woods because the Russian response will be rapid.

According to Major Stauffer, this flag story was Marshal Schörner's invention. Interesting that Schoerner had moved his headquarters way back to the safety of Czechoslovakia.

- Beware of these guys. They are always very dangerous.

- Major, soon all this madness will end. The Germany that Bismarck created seventy-four years ago will be a heap of smoldering ruins. Fire and brimstone is falling from the sky and had destroyed our Sodom. The Divine Providence which Hitler has claimed for himself throughout his life eventually will punish us.

- I wish I could say you are wrong but alas, you are only too right.

The night is calm. Around 5am I call the Gestapo guy and give him the order to choose a prominent tree. He looks at me speechless, "Why me?" "It's an order! If you refuse, I shoot you!" Willingly or unwillingly, he takes the flag and I accompany him to his tree, before taking my company into the woods.

Just when I was about to order my men to take their positions, Russian planes dive down on us determined to bury us under their bombs. Explosions everywhere, trees fall on us, our young soldiers scream, the older of the Home Guard paralyzed with fear, but this is just a taste of the symphony of death to come. They leave but ... my God! The T-34s are now only 400 yards in front of us, infantry clusters perched on top, others running alongside! They are charging straight at us!

I scream: "Everyone to last night's positions!" The platoon leaders and NCOs are trying to prevent some young soldiers from fleeing. I send an NCO, to fire on the Russians sitting on their tanks. The other gun was under the command of a platoon leader. That's what I thought. The T-34s approach. I see at least six of them coming straight toward my company. The machine gun on my right starts firing but nothing from the one to my left. How is this possible? I send a corporal to find out. Meanwhile the tanks, unable to enter the woods, strafe us abundantly.

Suddenly, the youngest of my soldiers burst from his foxhole, brandishing his bazooka. He screams like a madman, calls for his mother and rushed to assault of the first T-34. He is cut into two by a single burst of a Russian gun. Rage in my heart, I wave to Schneider and an NCO to take two bazookas and our assault rifle. Hidden by trees, we get closer to the T-34. I fire against a tank before me. The rocket explodes. Without leaving a second for the Russians to react, I shoot again. The explosion is even more terrible. To make sure their infantry cannot intervene I spray the Russian soldiers with my assault rifle. Other T-34s continue to fire blindly into the woods where some scared Home Guard soldiers start to flee. I scream: "Stay in your fox hole!" Totally panicked, they do not listen to me and are mercilessly mowed down like rabbits.

My corporal moves close to another T-34, hits its chains and immobilizes the tank. As the tank crew tries to get out they are mercilessly cut down one after the other with our assault rifles. The remaining tanks flee, passing some of our positions. Two of them are hit by our bazookas. It's a stampede. We counter attack up to the edge of the woods and cut down much of their infantry. Their attack was repelled. I yell orders to fall back to our inside positions, because Russian artillery or their planes can intervene any time.

*

I need to know why the machine gun on my left has not done its job. The corporal I had sent comes back horrified:

- Lieutenant, I've seen a lot of massacres but this is beyond everything. They were hit by a bomb, three soldiers and the machine gun are a pile of flesh and metal. When I saw it, I picked up a bazooka that one of our 'valiant' fighters forgot to take with him when he fled the scene and I aimed it at the T-34 before me. It ended in a terrible explosion.

- Congratulations! Without you and other old timers, we would not be alive. But where's the sergeant?

We find him lifeless, a bazooka at his side. So it was he who had gotten the fifth T-34. Corporal Schneider takes off the man's jacket and examines his injuries: "Lieutenant, he was shot in the back twice! Look at where the bullet holes: two small holes in the back and on his front, two large exit holes that have shredded the skin. He was killed by one of us!" We call the old Home Guard man to join us. I commend him for his courage and ask:

- Were you in the platoon with the dead sergeant?
- Yes.
- Okay, but did the sergeant have problems with his group?
  No answer.

- You will stay with Corporal Schneider. And for all of us, absolute silence, not a word of this business!

Beside us, Wolfgang's company had fought valiantly. Now everywhere there is calm. I order my company platoon leaders to make an initial assessment. My company has lost fourteen men, including a platoon leader and a sergeant. Eight more were wounded, two very serious. I give the order to organize a first aid service. I wanted to find Wolfgang. After a while I came across one of his adjutants:

- Where's your company commander?
- Killed in the first air attack.
- You had dug trenches?
- Yes, and correctly placed our guns. But immediately after the air attack, their tanks came with their infantry. I took command, unfortunately, too late, the T-34 decimated us, their infantry penetrated the woods, it turned into hand-to-hand fight. The last T-34s managed to escape.
- Why did you let them go?
- Because we had no more ammunition!
- Same for us. Where's your company commander?
- Follow me, he is not far.

Then I saw Wolfgang. Both of his legs were blown off, the body dripping with blood all over. I knelt beside him, made a sign of the cross on his forehead and prayed aloud: "Wolfgang, my friend, God may have wanted to spare you at the end of the war and that I may follow you. May He forgive you your sins and grant you eternal peace."

I took his identity tag and I stood up thinking of the words I spoke in the morning: "Let us pray to God that we are still alive tonight." The sergeant who had led me to Wolfgang and several soldiers surrounded me.

- Comrades, the war is not over. And you, adjutant, what's your name?

- Warrant Officer Meier, lieutenant.

- Take command of the company and draw up an inventory of men and equipment. I'll get our battalion commander.

I had hardly made it to headquarters when Major Stauffer gives me the latest news:

- The Red Army closed the border behind us. They are already in northwestern Czechoslovakia.

- Major, we lost many men. The head of the 2nd Company, my friend Wolfgang, was killed. We have no nurses or medics for the wounded. We must act. This is urgent. We need to arrange a meeting with the colonel. I will return to the two companies to take care of the soldiers. Major, we must keep a clear head and keep up morale, the only way to save as many of our comrades as possible.

- You are right. I will immediately take care of finding nurses.

I was hoping for a burst of energy but I suddenly felt overcome by a deep feeling of hopelessness and a crushing fatigue. My God! How would this end? I took my water bottle and greedily drank the few drops of water that were left. Then I put one foot before the other with great effort, like a robot. Every time I came across a fallen soldier there was another moment of despair. The old Home Guard fellow was slightly injured and pleaded to be taken care of. I was drowning in the same desperate pleas of the many wounded. There was no help in sight, but I had to give them some answers. Tired as I was, it was my duty, to give them some form of encouragement. I promised that the battalion would soon send nurses. I was trying to get each one's story:

- To which company do you belong?

- To the second, lieutenant.

- Very well, I will help you get back there.

When we find the 2nd Company, Warrant Officer Meier was surrounded by two NCOs:

- Lieutenant, we lost at least half of our company. It's terrible.

He was a man totally overwhelmed by the disaster. Whatever was left of my energy and courage began to abandon me, too, but I said:

"Officer Meier, we all have gone through similar calamities. The difference is that those were not right at the end of the war. I expect that the nurses will arrive any moment to take care of the wounded. As for the dead, we will put them in mass graves. Note their names. I am leaving for my company to hear the latest news."

As I leave them, the nurses arrive. Relief. Here is the Major:

"The colonel will meet tomorrow with the battalion commanders and all company officers. Trucks should arrive around 9pm to take the wounded to a hospital. As to the dead, the usual instructions. In an hour a cold meal and water we will be delivered. At 10pm our battalion will head for a new defense line 12 miles from here."

At nightfall, trucks with the wounded left for a field hospital behind our new line of defense. I order warrant officers and NCOs to collect all the weapons and ammunition. Then we counted our soldiers including those disabled. From our two companies with 194 men we have only 92 left. Major Stauffer joined us and we leave. The sweetness of the night with its thousands of stars tells us that spring may be coming, but not for us.

This ignoble affair of the murder of our sergeant while he attacked the Russians would not leave my mind. I had to open up to the Major. I told him the story and concluded that I suspected that our Gestapo guy was the killer.

"One of the old Home Guard men was a part of the same platoon with the Gestapo guy and their leader was precisely the assassinated NCO. I propose that we let the troupes take a rest in about an hour. When we resume our march we will place Corporal Schneider next to the old Guard man at the end of our column. There they can talk without being overheard. I believe that man knows a lot."

- Okay, we will stop for a short rest in an hour. I will tell the men that tomorrow we will probably have our first hot meal in four days. It is important that we do not allow any of the Nazis to escape.

- Especially because they would desert to the Russians and give them information about our strengths and weaknesses.

*

We arrive at our rest stop at dawn. First the hot meal that we had missed for four long days. Relief showed on our soldier's tired faces. I move a bit away from them to have a private conversation with the Major.

"My dear Aloys, we have gone through some truly awful days together. Tomorrow at 8am we will have a meeting with our colonel while your two companies will rest. I somehow do not think that today we will see any Russians".

A number of officers had assembled at headquarters, some familiar, some unknown to us. After welcoming us, Colonel Hausenberger gets right to the issues at hand:

"First: our division commander, Major General Nagel has gone back to rejoin Marshal Schörner's staff.

Second: he appointed me commander of the division and of our artillery regiment, and all the rest of our defense forces. We don't have many vehicles left but enough fuel to enable us to take off at the end of the war. As a fine surprise we just received a rocket launching battery which is even better than the Russian 'Stalin organs'. This will be our last message to the Soviets when they attack us next.

Third: currently, the 78th Division, the artillery regiment and the rest have about 15,000 men, but there are still two or more divisions around Zittau, on the border with Czechoslovakia.

Now some news to be taken 'with a grain of salt': Churchill had suggested to the Americans to enlist the officers and soldiers of the Wehrmacht, even the Waffen-SS, to continue fighting the Soviet Union to put an end to the last dictator in Europe.

According to what I found in the papers left by Major General Nagel the war should officially end on the 7th or 8th of May. At division headquarters I uncovered a supply of spring camouflage jackets and a large stock of food, water, beer and a bit of white wine. We will share all that with our men. I would like to congratulate you and your men for successfully attacking T-34 tanks with our bazookas. Not so long ago you would have received a special military decoration for such acts of heroism. Today there is nothing left, no promotions or decorations. In Berlin, the Russians are at the gates of Hitler's bunker. For all of us, there is only one thing left to do: fight for our survival and that of our comrades."

I raise my hand. Any problem?

- Colonel, what are we going to do with the Gestapo men in our ranks?

Silence. Then the verdict:

- You arrest them. They will be brought before a military court to be hanged, using Marshal Schörner's methods.

The meeting ended. The battalion and company commanders are about to leave, except the regimental commanders are asked to stay with the colonel. I can't resist speaking up:

- Major, now that it's all over, there remains the hope that a new Germany will be reborn and become a free and modern democracy, following the example of the United States. Let's hope we can become a part of this!

- We're not there yet, Aloys, for sure. There are urgent things to do right now. We must think about regrouping the battalion. We will form two companies: I will take command of the first and you the second. We have eight days left to find a way to survive. Camouflage jackets will come in handy.

As decided the two companies are formed. The Major explains to the soldiers our positioning in the new formation. We begin to dig trenches, wherever possible under a tree or some other natural protection. The artillery, rocket launchers and flak cannons are put in place behind us.

By late afternoon, another hot meal and beer lifts the spirits of the fighters. At night, we place several advance observation posts. Nothing moves. The next day, only a few planes fly over us, still nothing to report. On May 1, a spy plane slowly moves to the left and behind us and then disappears. The Major tells me he spotted his Gestapo man. His execution will take place during the next attack. We agree. The small town behind is called Hermannstadt. This will be our last stop.

*

On May 2, 1945 at dawn the Russian artillery fires on us but our rocket launchers fight back, much to the surprise of the Soviets who immediately cease their fire. However, our regiment and our companies have again suffered casualties from their shelling. More deaths and injuries.

The two Gestapo guys are eliminated. I ask my 'guardian angel' whether it was he who had done it. No, it's the old Home Guard guy who rid us of the Gestapos, and for two reasons. First to avenge his NCO, but also to ensure his own safety because he had become an inconvenient witness. Corporal Schneider brought the traitors' papers and their Gestapo ID cards, one in the name of Doormann of the Home Guard, and the other certifying that he had full powers to defend the interests of our Führer Adolf Hitler. Full powers! No one can become his victim anymore ...

The number of wounded was becoming a real problem. We could not keep them with us. I propose to Stauffer to take over a building in Hermannstadt and to turn it into a hospital for our wounded, awaiting the arrival of the Russians. It should be an easily identifiable house with red crosses painted all over. The Russians would not kill the wounded, we believe. They would have a good chance of being sent home.

On May 3, we occupy our new line of defense at the perimeter of Hermannstadt. Luckily, we find that this city still has a well-equipped hospital, run by a doctor who has not fled. No need to look for another place. The doctor warns us that the city is still under Nazis control, but they have agreed to accept our wounded.

- How many Nazis are at the head of this administration?

- There is the County Party Chief and his adjutant.

- Ah! Our famous golden pheasants!

- Oh yes, indeed!

He laughed heartily and we thank him for the valuable information. According to an officer we met at the hospital, the division headquarters was a mile further away, on the other side of Hermannstadt, in a large farmhouse surrounded by trees. Ideal for camouflaging trucks, equipment, food .... Always good to know, even better to see. Colonel Hausenberger received us without delay. The Major told him about our dealings with the Hermannstadt hospital. He knows because he already had received the visit of local Party Chief and his adjutant:

- They are lunatics, capable of anything. Beware! And now the latest news. Our two super-Nazis Schörner and Nagel have abandoned their posts and have fled in plain clothes to join the Americans via Austria. Two or more divisions, near Zittau, crossed the border and are now in the Czech Republic. We are the last troops still present in this part of Germany. I have already started to organize our departure via Czechoslovakia.

- Colonel, do we still have some operational rocket launchers? and Flak? And bazookas? How about ammunition for the MG 42?

- If there is a final Russian attack we can respond with our latest rockets. That's all. You will have all the instructions for our departure tomorrow.

We salute one last time with the ritual "Heil Hitler!"

*

Now we know for certain that the war is indeed over. In the evening, a great hot meal is waiting for us, with beer and even a few bottles of white wine. The night is calm.

May 4, a quiet sunny day with only one thing to do: organize our departure. The Major and I decide to go for a ride into town where we see the two 'golden pheasants', the each armed with submachine guns:

- "Heil Hitler!" Do you have news from our Führer and his headquarters in Berlin?

- No, not at the moment. But we learned that the Bolsheviks suffered terrible losses and Berlin will be freed shortly.

- Ah! Good news, thank you, and "Heil Hitler!"

What good to chat longer with such crazy guys? Better to go to the hospital. We wanted to know how many people were still in town. The doctor thought that half had left, but the 'golden pheasants' now were threatening anyone who wanted to get away.

- Don't worry, we'll take care of those two. Here's what you'll do: after we have left, gather some men and go to meet the Russians with white flags and tell them that there are no more German troops in the city. The people also should deploy white flags and come out to welcome the 'liberators'. You will show them the two dead bodies of the 'golden pheasants' with their weapons. Believe me, this is the only solution to save the city and its people. Are there any other Nazis around?

- Yes, but once you have gotten rid of these two leaders, there will be no more!

- Do you have a cemetery in town where we can properly bury our dead?

- The cemetery is just behind the church, but there is no priest!

- Why is this?

- He had stood up to the 'golden pheasants', and he now rests in the cemetery.

- We will be able to bury our dead ourselves if we have to. Do not fear and do not talk to anyone.

Back with our companies, we called on the platoon leaders to establish order. Some of the soldiers, in their euphoria about the coming end of the war had lowered their guard.

- My dear comrades, just yesterday I told you that the war is not over yet and if our defense line was spotted because of your carelessness we risk the worst tonight or tomorrow.

- Lieutenant, we have not seen anything, not even a surveillance plane.

- The Russians are perhaps just cautious. Probably they have placed observation posts and we are being watched. Everyone must remain hidden. Tonight, you will place three observation posts 300 yards in front of our lines.

This development unnerved me. My guys had committed serious indiscretions. I was sure we would see ...

Around 9.30 that evening a horse drawn cart arrived with a good vegetable soup, potatoes, meat, bread, beer and water, even liver pate for our morning sandwich. Taking the cart driver aside I asked him to keep his cart and horses here as we might need them later.

The head of the first platoon had already sent some men to the observation posts. All this seemed to be going in the direction of prudence. I put on my camouflage jacket and lay on a blanket next to a fox hole. Sleeping in wartime is not real sleep, it is simply a lower degree of being awake. The night was quiet and in the morning, I could admire the sunrise on what promised to be a another beautiful day in May 1945.

A time to take it easy.

The sound of an engine makes us perk up. I get my binoculars out and scan the sky. The spy plane is there, on the left, flying over the city and above our line of defense.

- Major, if the Russians do not show themselves in one hour, fine. But I prefer that everyone is placed on alert.

No need to wait a whole hour. "Take cover!" The first shells rain down on us. I see the Major running to the shelter. There is nothing more to do than to hole up and try to survive fifteen minutes of relentless shelling. The burst never seems to end, one round of shells after the other.

Our rockets finally respond with a terrifying whistle and stop the Russian artillery, giving way to the screams of the wounded. This is terrible. In total dismay I shed tears of utter fury! I am at the end of my wits. I speak to God: why have you abandoned us? A moment of absolute despair, interrupted by a sergeant from the 1st company: "Lieutenant! The Major is hit! Come!"

The Major was bleeding badly. Someone had already bandaged him and made a tourniquet to stop the bleeding. His left leg was torn off below the knee and he had numerous injuries all over his body. The sergeant had sent another comrade to the hospital to look for nurses.

It was a frantic race for time by the women and men in white coats led by the Red Cross hoping that the Russians let us take care of our wounded and our dead. In my company, one of my platoon leaders had already gathered the seriously injured. The nurses were working feverishly. We found out that the Russian artillery had concentrated its fire on one side our defense line. They had been 'tapping in the dark' but somehow did find our lines with the massacre guaranteed! A major from division headquarters comes running:

- Where is Major Stauffer?
- Seriously injured, currently on the way to hospital.
- In this case, can you replace him tomorrow at a meeting with the division commander?
- Yes, Major.

- We can send a truck to transport the dead, because I think you want to bury them.

- Yes, Major, thank you for sending a truck! See you tomorrow.

My company still had a warrant officer, two NCOs, my Corporal Schneider, and 18 Home Guard men. The truck arrived late evening. The bodies of our comrades, horribly mutilated, some in pieces, were loaded together, a vision of horror! They were buried the next day at dawn, in a corner of the cemetery, in the presence of a man who introduced himself as the mayor of the city. He promised to enter the list of the dead in his official records. I was surprised by his initiative but the man explained that he was a friend of the doctor who had told him about me. There were now a dozen locals ready to meet the Russian army. It was the 7th of May 1945.

The survivors of our two companies had gathered on the town hall square. A hot meal was to be delivered in an hour, giving me time to go to the hospital. Major Stauffer was on the second floor. I followed the doctor while telling him about my meeting with the mayor:

- A man who is on your side.

- I know, but tell me, lieutenant, do you have any nurses available for us?

- I think yes. In an hour I will be meeting with our division commander and I will ask him.

Major Stauffer looked very pale. Luckily, they had found a nurse with the same blood type for an immediate transfusion.

- Major, sir ...

- No, my dear Aloÿs, call me Daniel. I do not know how to thank you for everything you have done. With any luck, I'll find my family in the coming months. Give me your parents' address. Once the mail is working again, I'll write to them.

- Thank you, Daniel. Maybe we'll see each other again in a new Germany.

With a mixture of sadness and hope in our eyes, we looked at each other for a moment. Then, on a last hand shake, I left his bedside. No time to see the others.

Accompanied by my 'guardian angel' I went to headquarters. The colonel was waiting for me with the surviving officers:

"Comrades, as of today, May 8, the war is over. According to the instructions given by the victors, we must stay together and put down our arms. We will be prisoners of war. In our case we are prisoners of the Red Army. I think we can have a chance to escape this fate by crossing Czechoslovakia into Austria. Tomorrow morning, we will destroy our heavy weapons and retain only our small arms. Major Reinhard will handle the distribution of food. Each battalion will get a good hot meal before our departure. Please tell Major Reinhard the number of survivors of your battalion. As we have many injured, I sent our fourteen nurses to the hospital. They may have a chance to get back to their native region before we do. Tomorrow morning, the division will leave for Zittau. The Stauffer battalion under the command of Lieutenant Pappert will be the last unit to leave Hermannstadt early in the afternoon because Lieutenant Pappert knows how to deal with the city officials to make them surrender properly to the Russians. I wish you good luck and safe return your families."

Then the colonel came up to me to shake my hand:

- Major Stauffer told me much about you. Under normal conditions you would be named captain with great distinction, and this at the age of only 20!

- Colonel, the war ends tomorrow at midnight. Pray to God to be alive. Do we have the promised trucks for tomorrow?

- Yes, you will find six trucks behind the railway bridge with drivers and enough fuel. Start tomorrow afternoon. You will see a dirt road outside the big farm house and from there, you walk 100 yards passing under the bridge. Your trucks will be there, to your right.

- Thank you, sir.

All that was left to do was to find the rest of my battalion, a big word to describe all of twenty-three soldiers! They had not moved from the square in front of the town hall. The mayor was at my side while I transmitted the colonel's final instructions for our departure: "Within an hour we will have our last hot meal and sandwiches for the next day. Our objective is to drive across Czechoslovakia into Bavaria to surrender to the Americans. We will start tomorrow morning."

An old Home Guard man raises his hand:

- Lieutenant, I think we will find Czech partisans on the way. What are we going to do?

- Very good question. But tell me first what weapons you still have?

- Our assault rifles with some ammunition.

- Nothing else? I repeat: nothing?

Unanimous confirmation.

- When we walked into town, did you throw away any weapon, a bazooka or a pistol or any other?

- I had thrown away a bazooka before arriving in town.

"All right, tomorrow afternoon, when the Russians will enter the town it is very important that they will not find any weapons. If they do it will have very serious consequences for the towns people. When we cross the border we certainly will meet Czech partisans. If they attack us we will retaliate with our rifles. You will wait for my orders. Another question?"

The mayor stepped in to offer us tables and chairs from the neighboring buildings so that the soldiers could take their last meal in some comfort. I thanked him and apologized for not remaining with them: "I'll take a ride to the hospital to visit the wounded. After that we'll join you for this last hot meal. Make sure the soldier with his cart and horses does not leave. I absolutely must talk to him."

I did not move without my camouflage jacket. At the hospital, I saw most of my company's wounded. Two of the less severely wounded were determined to leave the hospital, pleading with me to take them with us. The doctor told them they would need four to six weeks for complete recovery but they did not want to be taken prisoners by the Russians. Before answering I wanted to see the doctor. Many of the other wounded did not have as much luck as those two. Some were very badly cut up, some were dying, not recognizing me. Had I really done everything I could to save them? I felt a sense of guilt rising in me. No! I had done everything, everything that was in my power. I struggled not to be drawn into an emotional abyss. You are responsible for the living! The mayor surprised me in the middle of my torment: "Is everything alright, sir?" I had regained control of myself: "Yes, let's go to this meal on the square."

At 8pm my brave soldiers had already settled around the tables in a rather relaxed atmosphere. My adjutant asks me to sit beside him. I invite the mayor to join us and he accepts with pleasure. According to my adjutant, the soldier who had brought our hot meal will return in two hours with more food for the coming days. "Fine, I'll be there." The mayor is thrilled:

- Very good food and beer! For at least two months I have not had a drop of beer! There are many villages around the city, we never went hungry. But the Zittau brewery that supplied us before now only serves the army.

- Maybe after tomorrow you may have occasion to drink with the Russians..... Mr. Mayor, would there be a way to let my soldiers sleep inside, even on the floor?

Without hesitation, he agrees to prepare sleeping quarters inside the town hall. I return to the hospital. I have only a half an hour. I made my decision for my two wounded soldiers. They were young, they had overcome being fanatics, now they are fighting for their lives. I asked the nurse to renew their bandages tomorrow morning before 10am, because I will then come and get them. They will go with us.

- Does the doctor know?

- Yes, I am well aware that they still have difficulty walking but I have a horse and a cart to get them.

- At your orders, sir.

- You were with our division?

- Yes, Lieutenant, 14th regiment.

On the town hall square, there were lively conversations. We talked about the future. It was crazy... Watching them, I thought of the parable of the child that our old priest used often in his homilies: "Lord, you are here! Today is already a piece of heaven!" I was moved and very happy. Let the peace come whenever it please you! The driver of the horse cart yanks me out of my reverie that could have easily turned into anxiety. My adjutant had distributed boxes with food for the next day and had reserved two beers for the mayor and me. I had in mind to toast a little later with him. The man with the cart wanted to know more:

- Lieutenant, what's my schedule for tomorrow morning?

- I expect you here at 11am. We will use your cart to move two wounded to the trucks.

- You know the way, sir?

- Yes, of course.

- If you do not mind, lieutenant, can I stay here with you? I have no more duties at the division. They all will leave for Zittau early tomorrow morning. Major Reinhard had asked me to be sure that the destruction of heavy equipment will be with a minimum of noise. He hopes to see you in Zittau.

- Very good. Did you have supper? - Yes.

- You see the platoon chief over there? Go and introduce yourself to him. You will stay with my company. Do you have everything needed for your horses?

The mayor is holding the two bottles of beer in his hands.

- Let's have them at my home. I will introduce you to my wife and my daughter.

I apologize for not having brought him more than just two bottles. No problem, his wife and daughter do not drink beer, water will do.

- Do you have other children?

- Yes, two sons, perhaps same age as you?

- I am twenty.

- Twenty! I have observed you ever since you came to this city. I am so impressed with your command of the situation, with your wisdom in making your decisions and your concern for your soldiers and for us.

- Mayor, the war forges one's character. Since I am a devout Catholic my conduct has always been guided by my faith in God. This may sound a bit pompous to you but it is the truth. That is why the well being of my soldiers is as important to me as my own.

After a long silence:

- I had two sons, they would be 29 and 27 now. One was at Stalingrad, and we have not hear from him since. The other fell at Normandy, 'for Hitler and the Fatherland'.

What could I say? The was a moment of quiet contemplation.

The mayor invited me to sleep at his home but I declined his offer. I wanted more than anything to spend the last night with my war comrades.

They all were lying on the floor in the town hall, ready for a restful night. The adjutant asks:

- Lieutenant, what is the schedule for tomorrow?

- Don't worry about it, just go to sleep. The mayor and the people will protect us. By the way, what's your name?

- Warrant Officer Heiner Feldmann, sir.

The deputy mayor brought towels and even soap. During your absence, I went to the hospital to get water bottles for tomorrow.

- Well done, and thank you. And now, good night.

*

May 8, 1945.

When I open my eyes my watch says 6.30am. I had taken my boots off for the night and tiptoed the bathroom to wash. No matter how much I tried to move quietly, I woke up my adjudant.

I gestured for him to remain silent and to go freshen up. In my backpack, I still had a clean pair of socks and changed. I was ready to face the last day of the war. Downstairs, tables and chairs were still there, perfect for a good breakfast. The mayor was already there:

- What time do you have breakfast?
- Around 8am! Everyone will be ready.
- Our women made coffee, 'ersatz', of course, but it is something warm, and toast with jam. Your men will not have to tap into their rations right now.
- Mr. Mayor, thank you from my all my heart, it will be a pleasant surprise for all of us.

Upstairs everyone was milling around. I called adjutant Heiner:

- Everybody down at 8, and be sure that no one forgets his gear because we will not go back up again. Breakfast will be served at 8am sharp. A surprise from the mayor, but hush...

The breakfast was excellent, the soldiers's spirits rising high. At 9am I went with the cart driver to get the two wounded soldiers. While the nurses helped them down, I went to thank the doctor. He accompanied me to bid farewell to Major Stauffer. He was happy to see me:

- Today I will pray for you, for this day and all others.

These words of a friend and a Christian one made me very emotional. I gave him a big hug:

- Daniel, I will never forget you.

I turned around. I did not want him to see my tears.

At ten, what remains of my company listen to me:

"Comrades, the war is over as of midnight. Our division has already left this morning for Zittau. God willing, we shall meet up with them this evening at the latest. Get your rifles, the rest of your ammunition and your food. Take nothing else. Leaving the city, we will not take the highway to Zittau but will cut across the fields to go under the railway bridge where six trucks are waiting for us. We will all go into the last two, the other trucks will pick up our comrades that have gotten lost and were separated from their units. We must save them."

At 10.30 sharp: "Forward march!" I am leading my company out of Herrmannstadt, followed closely by my 'guardian angel'. Suddenly the two 'golden pheasants' appear, submachine guns in hand. They threaten us and yell: "Go back to the front immediately." I tell them: "The war is over, we leave the city to save its inhabitants." At these words, they take aim at us. A hail of fire from behind me cut them down. My 'guardian angel' had spoken with his rifle. I walked over to the two Nazis lying there and with my 7.65 I put a bullet between their eyes. I turn to my soldiers with a sarcastic sort of eulogy: "The cult of Hitler's 'Providence' and the Nazis ended today in Hermannstadt on the 8th of May, 1945 at 10.45am!"

What a great relief! I finally feel liberated from Nazism. Corporal Schneider looks at me with a big smile and I say: "Thank you, my friend. You saved my life and those of many others."

The mayor and some towns people had watched the scene from a distance. I shouted to them: "I leave you the 'golden pheasants'. The Russians will love their uniforms. Tell them that this is our last gift to them!"

The farm was not far off. We already see the railway bridge I ask adjutant Heiner and his soldiers to cut through the fields to get to the trucks as fast as possible. The cart with the two wounded and Corporal Schneider take the dirt road. See you soon!

As we pass the farm, I take one last look at Hermannstadt. What! I see a T-34, majestically punctuating the street emanating from the city. He almost seems to taunt us, saying loud and clear: "We are the victors!" Then I see him direct his gun in our direction. This cannot be true! I scream: "Holy Virgin, protect us!" A bright flash, and then the explosion.

Frozen in place, petrified, everything around me is nothing but a tornado of flesh and blood and debris. I hear screams, they come from the railway bridge. My 'guardian angel' lying on the ground in front of me. Corporal Schneider ... I hoist him on my back and start to run towards the bridge like a robot. Suddenly some arms raised me up, someone is talking to me, they call me, sir! sir! Lieutenant! And then nothing but a black hole.

When I regained consciousness I found myself in a slow moving truck. It was the afternoon of May 8, 1945. Gradually I could make out the faces of my adjutant Heiner and of some others that I recognized. They said that they were seeing something like a miracle! I vaguely remember to have been hoisted on this truck.

- Lieutenant, do you remember the cart with the wounded and with Corporal Schneider?

- Yes, vaguely.

- The T34 fired at it. It was a massacre! Corporal Schneider died instantly. You were covered with blood and pieces of flesh. You carried the body of the corporal on your back. We came to your help, and we saw that the corporal had died, so we loaded you on the truck. When we started to clean you up we were sure to find lots of injuries. But nothing, absolutely nothing! In the midst of an explosion and not a scratch! Lieutenant, this is like a real miracle!

I said nothing, but I thanked the Virgin Mary, convinced that she had protected me again.

Our trucks continued as fast as we could in the direction of Czechoslovakia hoping to find the Americans so that we could surrender to them.

This time, luck would not be on our side.

Instead, we would find ourselves on a journey into hell.

*

Post-Script

Aloysius Pappert's "A Stolen Youth" is a very moving and emotionally charged account of a young German coming of age under the harsh dictatorship of the Nazi party and his journey from boyhood to the inferno of World War II.

His is not a book about generals or grand strategy, nor is it a story of the 'little man' powerless in a world not of his making. What makes Aloysius' story so remarkable is how a young man was growing into a position of leadership where he had to make many painful decisions about the lives and the welfare of the soldiers entrusted to him. What helped him in this most remarkable journey was his unbending conviction that following his Faith would give him the courage to doing what is right. And this he did, and so he reports about it so movingly.

I was honored that my friend Pappert asked me to translate his French manuscript. Both of us knew that this would not be an easy task. It is not enough to find the equivalent words in another language. It is also necessary to convey the emotions and the drama that are so well expressed in Pappert's original French. We wanted our readers to get the proper impression of the weight of Pappert's many traumatic experiences. Also, Pappert has his very own unique writing style that convincingly tells about dramatic situations in a way that the reader almost feels to be right there with the action.

For my attempts to find the right 'tone' it may have helped that I, too, had lived through World War II. Thankfully my own experiences with the horrors of war were nowhere near Aloysius' but certainly enough for me to appreciate how well he described what went on the lives and the minds of many Germans at that time. Aloÿsius wrote about this better than anyone I know.

Let us hope that my translation is doing justice to his "Memories from a War".

WOLFGANG MACK, PHD
SEATTLE WASHINGTON USA

Made in the USA
San Bernardino, CA
06 January 2017